FOREWORD

I have written this book in the light of most recent developments in many societies in the world. The key word to describe the new changes is globalization which seems to be a single word term conveniently describing all the complex technological, economical, political, and social changes happening not only in individual societies, but also on a global scale. Thanks to better communication and transportation technologies, the world really seems to be transforming itself into a global village. However, this is not happening smoothly and without any obstacles which seem to be caused by cultural barriers. The integration of the world into a single market in which there is freedom of movement of capital, goods, and services seem to be obstructed by groups who claim that these changes will affect their cultural values and identities in a negative way. This is not only happening in the nonWestern part of the globe, but in Western countries itself which struggles with controversial issues of the integration or assimilation of minorities into their societies. The world is basically facing two opposite processes:

globalization which implies integration of all countries in a global community and at the same time polarization caused by seemingly opposite cultural differences.

Culture is actually something which is a complex mixture of norms, values, roles, and goals. In time, persons living with each will other develop what is being called a distinct culture with exclusive values, beliefs, and thoughts. These non-material aspects of the social reality are actually social constructions by real persons. Unfortunately a process of reification happens which makes these cultural products separated from the day-to-day reality of those same persons who made those cultural products in the first place. Culture will then become a static phenomenon which cannot be changed. This rigid frame of mind will be reflected in the way people communicate: inflexible, intolerant, close-minded, and not facilitating any form of consensus. Culture has not only become exclusive in the minds of these people, but also intolerant because it is rejecting others who are not part of that particular culture. This static interpretation of culture has caused numerous problems like miscommunication and conflicts.

I wrote this book in the spirit of a different interpretation of culture. I do not believe in the close model of culture, because it is not a true reflection of the social reality. I have seen how people are capable of communicating in an open and positive atmosphere in which they do form meaningful relationships and reach consensus based on common values, beliefs, and thoughts. Based on my own experiences and observations, I can safely conclude that a lot of people interpret culture as a dynamic aspect in the social reality. In this dynamic interpretation of culture there is plenty of room for positive communication, sharing, learning, and creating a better world for all involved.

This book started as a series of online articles which I wrote over a period of two years. I was really happy to see the positive response from my readers which boosted my intention to expand those articles into this book. I want to thank Kendall Blair for editing this entire manuscript in a very professional manner. I hope that we will be able to work together on many other books I am planning to write in the near future. I also want to thank my wife and son for supporting me in writing this book. Last but not least, I want to thank my online readers who have given positive comments on my articles. I hope my offline readers will benefit in the same way.

Copyright

1st Edition 2018

ISBN: ISBN-13: 978-1986665506

ISBN-10: 198666550X

Visit our publishers website:

http://www.asian-europeanuniversity.com

Email:

info@asian-europeanuniversity.com

TABLE OF CONTENTS

A Formula for Effective Communication

FORMULA OF EFFECTIVE COMMUNICATION

Why are certain persons more successful than others in their personal lives and in their professional environment? Some are perhaps very successful at their homes, having good relationships with their spouses and children, but having many communication problems in their office: problems with bosses, but good relationships with co-workers or vice versa, good relationship with the bosses, but conflicts with other managers and subordinates. Others again are having good relationships at the office at the expense of their marriages and family life: too much time is being spent at the office and the family at home is being felt ignored and left behind.

The root cause of the problem is communication or to be more exact: *effective communication*. It is actually surprising that a lot of communication is going well most of the time. However, if a communication problem happens, the question: what went wrong? usually remains an unanswered question. There are plenty of books, articles and websites dedicated to the problems of communication. Some give scientific evidence of communication barriers and obstacles, but leave finding practical solutions to the reader. More practically oriented recipes are difficult to implement due to lack of time and practice.

For example the trait assertiveness: it has become common knowledge that it is important to be assertive in daily life. The issue of assertiveness is especially important in conflict resolution. The capacity to manage conflict is one of the most important skills you can possess in your personal and professional life. Conflict is caused by a clash of opinions, values or needs. It can be positive and constructive or negative and destructive, depending on the way people deal with it. Responses to conflict are learnt early in our childhood. These responses become habits and reactions used throughout our adult life. No matter where the source of conflict arises, or the level of conflict involved, the common key to conflict resolution is effective communication. People who are able to say what they mean and to acknowledge the rights of others to have opinions and feelings are effective communicators. They are assertive and thus better able to use a variety of communication strategies to resolve conflict.

Assertive behavior shows in your way of speaking, listening and questioning, and in your nonverbal behavior. This style of behavior is constructive and helpful when conflict arises because the needs of both parties are acknowledged and addressed. You are both more likely through this style of communication, to understand one another and the situation. Acting assertively in a conflict situation means standing up for your rights and expressing what you believe, feel and want in direct, honest and appropriate ways that respect the rights of the other person. Assertive behavior increases our self-esteem, leads to the development of mutual respect with others and helps us achieve our goals. Assertive behavior allows us to express our feelings in a way that is unlikely to lead to a defensive or aggressive response from the other person.

Two assertive people can express different points of view. The assertive person wants to be heard and acknowledged. This does not necessarily mean winning. It means being accepted and treated as an equal-respecting the rights of others and being respected in turn. Two assertive people can accept that each has a different opinion or perspective. When the occasion demands, assertive people can disagree; stand up for their rights and present alternative points of view without being intimidated or putting the other person down.

Assertive people realize the type of behavior suited a particular situation and recognize when their own behavior is assertive, aggressive or passive (see chapter 7).

But how can one be assertive if he or she is introvert by nature? Most people are familiar with Karl Jung's division of humanity into extraverts and introverts. The extraverted attitude is characterized by an interest in people and things and in relationships with events in the external world. The extravert is more concerned with outer reality than with inner fantasy, and tends to have scientific rather than metaphysical interests. The introverted attitude, on the other hand, prefers reflection to activity. The introverts tends to lack confidence in his relationship with people and things, and to be attracted more to philosophical than scientific interests.

On top of personality (extrovert versus introvert), there is the issue of culture: people from certain countries are simply less extrovert than from other countries. The comparison of national culture has been undertaken by Geert Hostede in his brilliant book *Cultures and Organizations, Software of the Mind* (1991). According to Hofstede, culture can be defined as the collective mental programming of the people in an environment. In this sense, culture is not a characteristic of individuals, but includes a number of people who were conditioned by the same education and life experience. These people then have a common collective mental programming. This programming is different from other groups, tribes, regions, minorities or majorities, or nations. Without going into a detailed explanation of Hofstede's fascinating book, he discovered that a country like the USA, like most other Western countries, is an individualistic oriented country where assertiveness is an important trait for both men and women. In an individualist society, everybody is supposed to take care of himself/herself and his/her immediate family. Identity is based on the individual and the emphasis is on individual initiative and achievement. In this society, everybody has a right to a private life and opinion.

The opposite of individualistic societies are so-called collectivist societies like Mexico and many other developing countries. In these societies, private life is invaded by organizations and clans to which one belongs. Opinions are predetermined. Belief is placed in group decisions and there is emotional dependence of individuals on organizations and institutions. It is not the assertive behavior which is sought after, but oftentimes the submissive behavior is perceived as being the ideal role in society. Submissiveness is completely the opposite of assertiveness and here it is obvious that national culture has a big impact of communication styles.

Wouldn't is be extremely useful to have a simple formula of effective communication which can be used in all circumstances? I think the following formula would be helpful:

EFFECTIVE COMMUNICATION=
SELF-INTEREST + INTEREST OF OTHERS – DISTUBING FACTORS OR
EC = SI + IO – DF
Let's look at the three elements of this formula.

When people communicate, self interest is probably the main reason for communication. One is far more interested in his or her own interest than in the interests of others. The above formula can actually be simplified even further by simply stating that communication is equal to self-interest. For this reason, communication is rarely effective because one is not trying to find a common ground in interaction processes but merely seeking a way to fulfill certain short-term interests. The most important problem in communication is probably asymmetry. The two parties in question are having different agendas and different interests which are further complicated by asymmetries of, knowledge, power and authority. For this reason, negotiation skills and tactics have become a very important trait of modern civilization. In the old days, physical strength was the determining factor to force the other party to compromise. Thanks to civilization, consensus can now be reached by communication. This civilizing process is basically a shift from a "command and control" communication culture to a "negotiating and persuasion" culture.

This shift has been argued in a persuasive manner by the famous sociologist Norbert Elias. In his book *The Civilizing Process* (2000), Elias attempts to understand and explain the process of civilization in Western societies. According to Elias the process of civilization was accompanied by the emergence of civilized behavior after the Middle Ages in Europe. Civilized behavior is only possible when people are forcing themselves to behave in a civilized manner. This can be illustrated by the ritual of eating meals. Nowadays, a knife, fork and plate are considered proper tools during consumptions of meals. This was not the case in medieval societies. After the establishment of kingdoms, taxation and violence have become monopolized by the state. This has stimulated the civilization process in an accelerated manner. Consequently, it became important to resolve conflicts by non-violent tools like manipulation, diplomacy, power, and knowledge.

The shift from a "command and control" communication culture to a "negotiating and persuasion" culture has resulted in a greater emphasis on the ability to effectively communicate verbally and non-verbally with each other. This also implies better education in which development of dialogue skills has become the backbone of modern education. People are at a young age already required to be able to express their thoughts clearly in class presentations, essays, reports and not to mention in theses of various sorts in tertiary educational settings.

INTEREST OF OTHERS

The interest of others has probably been the most important issue in many textbooks about effective communication. The ability to listen, to get and give feedback, to control anger ("anger management"), conflict resolution, stress management, etc., have been discussed in great lengths by many authors, scholars, management trainers, etc.

The problem is accommodating the interests of others have become more important with the introduction of information technology and the ability to trade goods and services in cyberspace. True globalization has probably already occurred in cyberspace where a global

24 hour economy has been created where everybody is exchanging goods, services and information all over the world.

Everybody has become a customer! It is important to look at the needs of others as your customer. This marketing concept was first used in transactional settings, but was introduced in learning organizations and now has become an important concept in all corners of life.

The traditional corporate structure, with its formal chain of command and division of labor, is undergoing massive changes in companies throughout the world. Changing markets and technological breakthroughs, now dictate the organizational structure most appropriate for a company. Firms that rely on the ability to introduce innovations continuously usually give employees more latitude for decision making and communication outside the formal chain of command. The new learning organization or also called the 'boundaryless' organization relies on self-managing work teams and the use of networking. It reduces or eliminates internal boundaries that separate functions and hierarchical levels. The learning organization is organized around core-customer oriented processes, with each process team comprised of various functional specialists.

The issue of discovering the interests of others has even been infiltrated by non-scientific 'tools' like astrology, numerology and tarot cards. Before the discovery of these tools, one was still utilizing (and still is utilizing) many scientific tools offered by psychologists ranging from psychoanalysis, conversation analysis, transactional analysis and the sort resulting in various therapies which might be effective depending on the willingness of the buyer to take it seriously or not.

How can one discover the interests of others? This requires a proactive approach from both parties. Two strategies might be helpful. The first strategy is called the *PAIR* approval strategy: Placate (listen, empathize, and respond with concern); Attend (to the other); Investigate (circumstances details of issue); Resolve (decide on action to take). The second strategy is called the five-step method: listen (be open-minded, remember), respond show concern and empathy and apologize for any inconvenience), decide on action (carefully think about the factors which might influence you), take action (act promptly) and follow up (confirm that the problem has been solved and the other person is happy).

In her excellent book titled *How To Talk So People Listen* (2006), Sonya Hamlin offers a very useful method to discover the interests of others. Hamlin argues that anyone can be reached by your message if you are able to make them listen to your message; it is extremely important to make others listen to what you have to say. Finding out anyone else's selfinterest is all about focus. There are basically three basic motivating factors that stimulate anyone to listen to any speaker: (!) What's in it for me?; (2) Who's telling?; How do you tell it? According to Hamlin, finding out the interests of others is not very difficult. To understand someone else's interests is simply analyzing what we all have in common in terms of goals, needs, and expectations.

DISTURBING FACTORS

The third element of effective communication is probably the most difficult one: how to eliminate disturbing factors or how to overcome communication barriers. There are basically six types of barriers between people communicating with each other: differences in perception, incorrect filtering, language problems, poor listening, differing emotional states, and differing backgrounds (see chapter 3). In order to overcome these barriers, one must be willing to avoid selective perception, condense messages to the bare essentials, use specific and accurate words possible, always verify your interpretation of what's been said, be aware of the feelings that arise in yourself and in others as you communicate, and attempt to control them.

Communication barriers also exist within organizations. Although all communication is subject to misunderstandings, business communication is particularly difficult. There are three distinct moments which can cause many communication barriers in organizations; during negotiations, when dealing with customers and clients, and holding meetings.

NEGOTIATIONS

Negotiating is something that most people have experienced in their lives. For instance, inquiring about an increase in salary or the price of a car. *Negotiation* can be definedas a process by which two or more interdependent parties use bargaining to reconcile their differences (Gordon, 1988).

According to Gordon (1998) the negotiating process demonstrates a fundamental tension between the *claiming* and *creating* of value. This institutes that *Value claimers* view negotiations simply as an adversarial process. An adversarial process is one that sets up a specific and focused conflict. Each side tries to *claim* as much of a limited pie as possible by giving the other side as little as possible. Each party claims value through the use of manipulative tactics, forcible arguments, limited concessions, and hard bargaining. *Value creators,* on the other hand, try to find a way which is beneficial for each party: a win-win solution.They try to find this win-win solution through emphasizing shared interests, developing a collaborative relationship, and negotiating in a cooperative manner.

Their main goal is *creating* additional benefits for each side in the negotiations.

There are basically two general strategies in negotiations: (1) *Distributive bargaining* which translates into a win-lose approach; (2) *Integrative bargaining* which translates into a problem-solving or win-win approach. A negotiator incorporates these strategies individually or in combination in one of two basic paradigms (Gordon, 1998). Distributive bargaining is the classical view. This bargaining is considers as a win-lose situation, where one party's gain is the other party's loss. Known also as a *zero-sum* type of negotiation (because one party's gain equals the other party's loss, thus a gain of zero), this approach characterizes the purchase of used cars, property, and other material goods in organizations. Salary negotiations and labor-management negotiations can also be put in this category..

Distributive bargaining highlights the claiming of value. Winning the negotiation in this case depends to a large extent on the choice of opening offers, the ability to influence the opponent to view the situation in a way favorable to the negotiator, and the careful planning of offers and counteroffers. It must be realized that power plays a key role is successful distributive bargaining. This is because power can increase a party's leverage and its ability to shape perceptions.

Recent research encourages negotiators to transform the bargaining into a win-win situation. This is known as *Integrative Bargaining*. Here, both parties gain as a result of the negotiation.

Integrative Bargaining is also known as a *positive-sum* type of negotiation, simply because the gains of each party yield a positive sum. This approach has recently characterized international negotiations, labor-management negotiations, and specific job-related bargaining.

Effective Communication Skills during Negotiations

1. *Be an alert negotiator.* A successful negotiator must be assertive and open to challenge everything. Skilled negotiators know that everything can be negotiated. Challenging is not synonymous with refusing all the offers given by an opponent. All offers must be analyzed separately. You must ask the right questions when an offer is given. This implies that you have to be critical about everything you read in the newspapers and see on television. You will not be able to negotiate if you cannot challenge the validity of the information exposed by your opponent. Being assertive means that you need to ask the right questions in order to gather all the information you need to know. You are also not willing to always "no" for an answer. Train yourself to hide your feelings of anxiety or anger. Let others know what you want without feeling threatened. Train yourself to use "I" messages. For example, change "I do not want you to do that" into "I feel uncomfortable when you do that." Realize that there is a big difference between assertiveness and aggressiveness. You need to become assertive when you defend your own interests while respecting the interests of others at the same time. If you do not show consideration in the interests of others, you will look aggressive. Assertiveness is part of effective negotiations.

2. *Be a good listener.* A good negotiator is like a detective. They often ask probing questions and then listen. The other negotiator will inform you about everything you need to know; the only you have to do is listen. Many conflicts can be solved easily if we try to learn to the words of others. We all much too often busy speaking and forget to listen to the words of others. You can become an effective listener by letting others speak. Follow the 70/30 rule: 70 percent of the time is used for listening and 30 percent for speaking. Stimulate the other negotiator to speak with open questions: these questions cannot be answered by simple "yes" or "no."

3. *Be prepared.* Acquire as much as possible information related to the negotiation at hand. What are their needs? What pressures are they experiencing? What kind of options do they have? Knowledge about all these will strengthen your position when facing the "opponent." In short, the more information you have, the more prepared you will be for the "war."

4. *Set a high target.* Good negotiators will set a high target to get the best out their negotiations. If you expect to get a lot, you will end up with a lot. A good negotiator is always optimistic. All sales persons usually ask for more than what they expect and all buyers will offer less than what they are willing to pay for.

5. *Always be patient.* If we want to persuade someone, we must be flexible with the time we have. Our patience will be advantageous if the other negotiator is in a hurry.

Always thin rationally. Do not be reckless in making important decisions. This will have a big impact on your future.

6. *Focus on satisfaction.* Help the other negotiator to become satisfied. Satisfaction means that their primary interests are fulfilled. Do not confuse the primary interests with their desires. Try to accommodate their needs.

7. *Do not make the first move.* The best way to find out the aspirations the other negotiators is to persuade them to make the first move. The might be asking less than you thought. If you start with an initial offer, you might be offering them more than they need.

8. *Do not accept the fist offer.* If accept the first offer, the other negotiators will think that they have won. They will be more satisfied when you refuse to accept their first offer. If you say "yes" to their first offer, they will think that the have successfully pushed you to the limits of your abilities.

9. *Do not make easy concessions.* If you make concessions, try to get the other negotiator to also make concessions in exchange. "I shall do this if you do that." This tactic will usually make your opponents uncomfortable. They will think that you are smart and have a strong position.

10. *Do not hesitate to back off.* Do not negotiate without options. Prepare yourself for the worst outcome. Prepare several options as alternative strategies you have during the negotiations. This will give you the chance to think and reconsider the offers of your opponents. If you lose, you can at least say to yourself that you have done your best in the negotiation process.

DEALING WITH CUSTOMERS

Dealing with customers can become a very difficult interaction because some customers are difficult to satisfy and difficult situations may arise (Dwyer, 1997). Customers expect a high level of service. If it is not provided, the end result may be loss of business. Sometimes you may feel there has suddenly been an increase in the number of difficult customers. These customers do not have to be lost. Deal with them professionally and they will continue to want your services.

One of the most important things organizations need to do is providing service to their customers. Organizations must nowadays focus on their customers' needs by making them feel comfortable and respected. By anticipating and meeting customer's needs for information, you can take action efficiently and courteously. The role of the organization is to service its customers. Your role as a member of staff providing that service is to focus on the needs and expectations of customers. To deliver quality customer service, you must be able to communicate effectively.

When the product and price in one organization are similar to those in another organization, the quality of the service is what makes the difference. The organization with the better service maintains and builds good will. It is able to meet the needs and expectations of its regular customers. Customers are then abler to enjoy the service package as well as the environment. Many companies take their regular customers for granted while they are the base of the business. If regular customers are taken for granted, they might become upset and this might become detrimental. You then have an unsatisfied customer who may complain or simply walk away. The needs and expectations of regular customers determine the quality of the service. Ensure that the first impression is positive and welcoming. This applies to both regular and potential customers. As a member of the staff your organization can only provide the level of service your weakest member provides.

Effective Communication Skills When Dealing With Customers' Complaints

1. *Understand the complaint.* Before you answer an angry customer, show that you have understood the problem of that customer. If the customer has explained his or her complaints you only need to repeat the problem and find a solution. If the customer complaints in writing, quote the words of the customer to show that you have carefully read their letter of complaint. Record all the relevant data with the customer in question like date of purchase, account number, previous contact with customer service, etc. If you still do not understand the problem, read tip number 2.

2. *Ask for clarification.* An angry customer might be unable to write their complaint clearly. You can ask the customer to clarify the problem: did the customer receive a broken product or did the customer receive the wrong product? You can also ask how the customer wants the problem to be solved. Does the customer want the product to be replaced or does he or she want his or her money back? If you cannot clarify the problem and offer the right solution, you can make the customer angrier.

3. *Personalize the response to the customer.* An angry customer will not be able to cool down if he or she feels that no one is there to listen to his or her complaint. Respond with the following: "Dear customer, thank you for your letter. We will solve your problem and we are happy to hear from you about it." So send a personal letter to convince them that their complaint has been recorded clearly. Always use the name of the customer and do not forget their gender and titles. Repeat the information from your company and integrate that with your message. "We are proud that you have selected us as your provider for six years and we want to continue serving you as our valued customer." Personalize your message with your name. The customer needs to know that there is a human being who trying to solve his or her problem.

4. *Say that you will solve the problem as soon as possible.* An angry customer just needs concrete actions. So you need to specify how you are going to solve the problem of that angry customer. If the solution is complex break it down into steps which are understandable. If possible, state when the problem will be solved. "We will send your new order tonight and it will be delivered to you at 10 am." Or "We are going to check the shipment of your order right now to find out what went wrong."

5. *If delivering a good message, say it first.* If you can make a customer happy, deliver the good message first and then show empathy. Good message: "We will refund your money with pleasure as you requested." Empathy:" We fully understand your frustration because you received your Christmas gift after Christmas." However, if you cannot make the customer happy because you have to say "no" to the customer, show empathy first and then deliver the "bad news." Empathy: "We understand your frustration because you received the Christmas present after Christmas." Bad news:

"We cannot refund your money because your order has passed the last date of our product warranty."

6. *Use positive and polite tone.* You might be tempted to use answer customer complaints with a similar harsh tone: "You have dropped your camera and it is not covered by our product warranty." Try not to make the problem worse by using the wrong tone because you will be flooded by more angry responses. Use polite and positive words: "Your camera seems to be broken because you dropped it and we are sorry to respond that we cannot replace it because our warranty only covers losses due to manufacturing mistakes."

7. *Avoid blaming the customer.* Try to replace all the "you" words with "I" or "we." Do not say or write: "We cannot process your order because you did not mention your address on the purchasing order form." Say or write: "We cannot process your order because we do not have your address."

8. *Recognize the customer's frustrations.* Maybe the customer's problem is not caused by your company or maybe you cannot solve the problem. But you can imagine the frustration of your customer. Empathize with your customer: "We know that whatever caused our server to malfunction has already caused problems at your office."

9. *Apologize when you made a mistake.* When your company made a mistake, apologize. Make your apology specific. Avoid saying: "We are sorry that you are confused due to your credit application." Instead say: "We apologize for putting the wrong date on your application. We will amend this error immediately."

10. *Satisfy your customer by offering something valuable.* If your company's policy allows you to give discounts, products, or gifts to angry customers, you can say: "We will give a 50 percent discount if you buy a new camera." Customer complaints in written form are more difficult to handle. You will not have the opportunity to hear or see the customer. It is still very important you handle the complaint professionally.

CONDUCTING MEETINGS

According to Dwyer (1997) meetings cover three main areas of responsibility: (1) to provide the policy and procedures; (2) to organize and run the meeting within its standing orders and formalities; (3) to expect the members participating in the decision making and initiating and implementing actions within the meeting's areas of expertise and interest. When these three areas of responsibility are implemented consistently, meetings will become effective because the executive and members will get the opportunity to create new ideas, solve problems and make democratic decisions.

Most managers spend large amounts of time in meetings with their subordinates and company officials. They work as members of cross-functional work teams or as participants in special task forces. Conducting productive meetings is a recurring major challenge to many managers. Many meetings are simple information sharing sessions. The information can then better be disseminated by a short memo or a quick telephone call. Many other meetings are conducted to solve complicated problems while basic fact-finding and research has not been finalized.

The first step in conducting quality meetings is to ensure that the information provided is the appropriate vehicle for the type of communication required. Effective Communication Skills for Conducting Meetings

1. Distribute the agenda of the meeting before the session starts. A memo is usually distributed among the participants containing the topics which will be discussed in the meeting session. Give all the participants a chance to share ideas about the topics which will be discussed during the meeting. Avoid determining too many topics for discussion. Be consistent with what you want to discuss in a particular meeting.

2. Invite all the relevant participants and decision makers. They will play an important role in the end decisions of the meeting in question.

3. Choose a suitable place for the meeting. Try to find a large place with the proper atmosphere and comfort. The right place will facilitate the exchange of messages and provide you the opportunity to say what is necessary.

4. Choose chairs with soft cushions with sufficient lighting.

5. Make minutes of the meeting and distribute it to the participants after the meeting.

Important aspects before a meeting

Determine whether the issues at stake deserve to be solved.

- Are those issues important enough?

- Do we have enough resources and time to solve those issues?

- Are willing to allocate our resources and time to solve those issues? ***Explain the purpose of the meeting.***

- Why do we have to discuss these issues?

- What do we expect from this meeting?

- What are our roles in the attempts to achieve the targets expected?

- What do we expect from this meeting in connection with the relationships we have with outsiders? ***Prepare yourself.***

- What kind of problem do I have in mind and why?

- How can I express the problem in question?

- Is the problem caused by others?

- Do I have the willingness to listen to the other participants in the meeting?

- How do I feel about the problem? How do the others feel about the problem? Can we control our emotions when talking about it? ***Approach the others.***

- Contact the others and determine a neutral place to have a meeting.

- Ask whether all concerned can attend the meeting at a certain time and place.

Important aspects during a meeting

- Treat everybody with respect.

- Be honest.

- Listen to other views and understand why their views are important to them

- Explain your views and wants.

- Control your emotions. Take a break if necessary.

- Be patient. The discussion might be going in circles at times. Try to listen more carefully.

- Brainstorm. Share your ideas to fulfill the needs of all.

- Make a decision supported by everyone and make a plan of implementation.

Important aspects after a meeting

- Make minutes to record the joint decisions made during the meeting.

- In case the meeting did not produce a joint decision, plan the next meeting. Note down what has been discussed and what still needs to be discussed in a next meeting. This is important to avoid repetition of the same discussions in a next meeting.

- Make an agenda for the next meeting.

- In case crucial joint decisions have been made, evaluate those decisions. Monitor the implementation of the decisions. In case of deviations make necessary corrections or conduct an emergency meeting.

COOPERATION IS THE KEY TO EFFECTIVE COMMUNICATION

Why is it so important to communicate? It is important because it is the cement that holds our society together. Without the ability to communicate, we would not be able to create a civilized society which provides order and stability needed to improve the quality of our lives. But what is truly effective communication? Much has been researched and written on this subject, but until now, the ability to really be able to communicate effectively seems to depend on factors difficult to replicate: talent, emotions, psychological willingness to communicate, and many other "subjective" factors. With all these limitations in mind, it is extremely difficult to find an objective and rational way or formula to be able to communicate objectively. Rules of etiquette have been developed over the centuries in order to facilitate non-violent communication between civilized people. These rules have indeed proved to be effective only if certain conditions can be met: sophisticated education of the population, an advanced economic system providing enough well-paying jobs and a social security system to protect the weakest members of the society. If these "external" conditions can be met, the communication between people becomes much more efficient because people are able to control their emotions and anger ("Anger Management").

If all these conditions are met, people will know the conditions to communicate effectively. However, the effectiveness of the communication is only one of the possibilities or options from which people can choose. Other options of ineffective communication will still be available.

The following table will clarify this:

Interest of others versus Self-interest	High self-interest	Low self-interest
High interest of others	Cooperation	Submission
Low interest of others	Domination	Ignorance

According to this table, two aspects are very important in communication: personal interest and the interest of others. The three interaction possibilities that are ineffective can be identified as: ignorance, submission and domination (see chapter 7). Only one mode of communication can be identified as being effective: *cooperation.*

What are the characteristics of cooperative people? When people communicate together they are really trying to find a consensus based on an *equal* relationship. Both engage themselves in a communication and interaction that is being symmetrical. Both modes of communication ineffective, domination and submission are both caused by the phenomenon of asymmetry.

Another important criterion is *trust.* Without trust, you cannot expect a fruitful collaboration or cooperation (see next section in this chapter). Trust is based on the ability of both sides to exercise integrity and reliability. How can we trust another person who did not tell the truth (non-integrity) and / or not keeping his word (unreliable)?

The last criterion, which is crucial to facilitate effective communication, is the *action* orientation. Communication is a process of exchange of words. However, if words are not meaningful and oriented towards improving something, it becomes an empty ritual. This is actually the case when the ignorant mode of communication is happening. The two sides are not really interested in each other, even worse; they are not interested in themselves.

The explanation above may seem obvious, but it says nothing about communication skills, one must possess in order to facilitate optimal communication results. Communication is a dynamic process. Unfortunately, the process can be stopped before it really begins. What follows can go wrong:

1. *To decide what to say in the communication process.* Many people make the mistake of trying to convey everything what he knows about a subject. Unfortunately, when a message is overloaded with too much information, it is difficult to absorb. Problems may arise because of trying to get your point across, deciding what to include and what to leave out, how much detail to provide, and what to monitor. If you try to explain something without first giving the receiver suitable background information, it will create confusion.

2. Creating a real message is difficult if you do not know how it will be used. This could be due to a *lack of familiarity with the other person (s).* You need to know something about the prejudices, education, age, status, and the style of your receiver to create a message effectively. Decisions on the content, organization, style and tone of your message will depend, at least to some extent, on the relationship between you and the other person (s). If you do not know the other person (s), you will be forced to make decisions in the dark.

3. *Lack of experience in speaking* can also prevent a person from developing effective messages. Some people have limited education, lack of aptitude, limited vocabulary, are uncertain about grammar, are frightened to communicate, and lack experience in using language. These problems can be solved by taking courses in communication, participating in communication training programs, read plenty of self-help books, join some association or organization to practice communication skills: anything positive to overcome lack of communication skills.

HABITS OF HIGHLY COOPERATIVE PERSONS

Interpersonal relationships are not static, but always changes. To maintain and deepen interpersonal relationships, changes require certain actions to restore equilibrium. There are several factors which are very important to maintain this equilibrium: *friendship, trust, supportiveness, open-mindedness.*

4. *Friendship.* Friendship fulfills the need for attention. Interpersonal relationships will be maintained if both sides agree about the level of friendship. The second factor is related to the agreement about who controls who? If both sides disagree about concluding, frequency of talking, deciding, domination, conflicts might arise. Conflicts are usually caused by both persons wanting to dominate and both persons not wanting to compromise. The third factor is related to the right responses: response

A must be followed by response B which follows logically after each other. For example, in a conversation, a question must be followed by an answer; a joke must be followed by laughter, etc. These responses are not only related to verbal messages, but also related to nonverbal messages. There are basically two types of responses: confirmation and disconfirmation. Confirmations reflect agreement between two persons while disconfirmations reflect disagreement between the two. Confirmations will lead to a closer friendship between persons while disconfirmations might lead to the dissolution of the friendship. The fourth factor is related to emotional compatibility during interpersonal communication. If two persons do not show the same type of emotions during interactions, one person might be ending the interaction.

5. *Trust.* Trust can be identified as the most important factor which influences interpersonal communication. If you can trust someone, predict his/her behavior, be sure that you will not be disadvantaged; you will be willing to open up yourself to that person. Trust determines interpersonal communication because it is difficult to trust someone if he or she closes him/herself from you. If a person is not willing to share their thoughts and feelings, you will not be able to understand this person. Trust is influenced by two important factors: self-esteem and authoritarianism. Persons with high self-esteem are more inclined to trust others. An authoritarian person will be inclined to distrust someone else. Moreover, trust will be facilitated by the willingness to accept another person, show empathy, and honesty.

6. *Supportiveness.* A person who shows a supportive attitude in interpersonal communication will lower his or her defensiveness. A person who is defensive will be uncompromising, dishonest, and not empathic. What are the characteristics of supportive persons? A supportive person will expose his or her feelings and opinions without judging the other person. Supportiveness is also show through the willingness to cooperate with another person to solve a problem. A supportive person is also a spontaneous person who is honest and does not hide his or her motives. Empathy is another trait of supportiveness; without empathy people will look like machines without feelings and attention. A supportive person does not show any signs of superiority because he or she wants to communicate in a symmetric way by showing respect to different views and opinions. Finally a supportive person is willing to change his or her point of view if new evidence shows that a change of opinion is necessary.

7. *Open-mindedness.* Open-mindedness strongly influences the quality of interpersonal communication. The opposite of an open-minded person is a dogmatic person. The differences between an open-minded person and a dogmatic person can be summarized in the table below.

Open-mindedness	Dogmatic
Judge messages objectively by using data logic	Judge messages with subjective motives and
Easily see differences, nuances, etc	Simplistic thinking (black and white)
Content oriented	Look for source of message instead of content of message

Look for information from various sources	Trust based on own subjective thoughts disregarding information from others
Ready to change opinions	Rigidly defends own beliefs
Shows understanding towards contradicting own beliefs.	Refuse, ignore, distort messages inconsistencies

Source: Rokeach, 1960

From the above table it is clear that open-minded persons are seeking non-defensive interpersonal communication events with other persons. Open-minded persons are better in controlling their fears, worries, low self-esteem, defensive experiences, etc. Open-minded persons do not feel threatened easily in interactions. They will always try to understand the messages of others.

The table below summarizes the habits of highly cooperative persons.

Habits of cooperative persons	Description of habit
Friendship	1. Agreement about the level of friendship. 2. Agreement about who controls who? 3. Proper verbal and nonverbal responses reflecting agreement between two persons. 4. Emotional compatibility of two persons.
Trust	1. Openly sharing thoughts and feelings. 2. High self-esteem. 3.Accepting others. 4. Empathy. 5. Honesty.
Supportiveness	1. Exposure of feelings and opinions without judging the other person. 2. Willingness to cooperate with another person to solve a problem. 3. Spontaneity without hiding motives. 4. Empathy 5. Showing respect to different views and opinions. 6. Willing to change point of view based on new evidence.

Open-mindedness	1. Judge messages objectively by using data and logic.
	2. Easily see differences, nuances, etc.
	3. Content oriented.
	4. Look for information from various sources.
	5. Ready to change opinions.
	6. Shows understanding towards inconsistencies.

OVERCOMING COMMUNICATION BARRIERS BETWEEN PEOPLE

Good communication is not one and the same with talking other people into accepting your point of view. Regardless of how well you express yourself, it is impractical to think that others will always agree with you. However, others will understand you if you communicate well. When you send a message, you intend to communicate meaning, but the message itself does not contain the meaning. The meaning will be formed by your own perception and the perception of your receiver. To understand one another, you and your receiver must share similar meanings of communication. For instance, gestures, tone of voice, and other symbols.

OVERCOMING PERCEPTION BARRIERS

In the modern world we are constantly bombarded with information 'packaged' in different forms like sights, sounds, scents, and so on. Our minds organize this stream of feelings into a mental map that represents our perception or reality. Perception can be defined as our individual interpretation of the world around us. In no case is the perception of a certain person the same as the world itself, just as no two maps are identical. As you view the world, your mind absorbs your experiences in a unique and personal way. Because people have different ideas, they will also have different perceptions. If you go to restaurant, for example, you might be impressed by the art hanging in the restaurant and the good food served. Another person might be impressed by the good parking space in front of the restaurant, but this person might not like the food served. This is caused by unique perceptions of individuals. So when two people experienced the same event like eating in the same restaurant, their mental images of that event will not be the same. As senders, we choose the details that seem important and focus our attention on the most significant and general. This process is known as *selective perception.* As receivers, we try to fit new details into our patterns that we already have.However, we have a strange habit of distorting information instead of rearranging patterns when we find out that a detail does not quite fit. Overcoming differences in perception may be difficult.For this reason it is important to predict how your message will be received by anticipating the receiver's reactions. You must always try to avoid misunderstandings by constantly reshaping your message. A lot people have the habit of applying a single solution to every communication problem while it is much more effective to find specific solutions to solve specific problems.It is necessary to always frame your messages in such a way that will have meaning for your listeners. In turn, you have to frame your own mind in such a way that you will find something useful in every message you receive.

OVERCOMING INFORMATION BARRIERS

Information which we receive is always 'filtered' or abbreviated resulting in changes of the original messages. In business, the filters between you and your receiver are many; executives, assistants, receptionists, answering machines, etc. Just getting through by telephone can take a week if you are calling someone who is protected by layers of gatekeepers. The biggest problem is what will happen to your message when it finally arrives at your receiver. It will be digested, distilled, and probably distorted. The same will happen to the messages sent to you which will also be translated by the same gatekeepers. The same can be said when playing the childhood game of 'Telephone'. One person starts with a specific message. It is whispered down the line from person to person. Finally, the last receiver repeats what they have heard. Nearly one hundred percent of the time the message is a jumbled mess. To overcome filtering barriers, try to establish more than one communication channel, try to eliminate the middlemen, and decrease distortion by condensing the information to the bare essentials.

OVERCOMING LANGUAGE BARRIERS

When choosing the words to develop your message, you are signaling to others that you are a member of a particular culture or subculture. This is implied by the tone and verbiage that you use. Each culture has its code in a sense. If you know the code, then you are or have been a part of that group. Your message will be experiencing barriers due to the nature of your code which consists of your language and vocabulary. For example, the language of a teacher differs from that of a police officer. This difference in their vocabularies will definitely have a profound impact on their capability to recognize and express ideas.

Barriers also exist because words can be interpreted in different ways. As we all know, language uses words as symbols to represent reality. This means that the word book can be automatically tied the physical thing that is a book. We might as well call a book a worm. Language is a random code that depends on shared definitions, but there's a limit to how completely any of us share the same meaning for a given word.

Words are not really precise on the literal or denotative level. People in the West usually agree on what a book is. However, your idea of a book is a composite of all the books you have ever read: novels, school textbooks, telephone directories, and self-help guides.Someone from another culture may have a different range of book experiences: comics, religious guides, and cooking manuals. While you both might agree on the general concept of a book, but the precise image in your minds differs.

The differences on the connotative or subjective level are much bigger. Here feelings play a significant role because you might interpret a book by your feelings about it. You may have very positive experiences reading books. The books you have read really made a difference in your life boosting your knowledge and facilitating your progress at school in your job. However, you might not be fond of books because you never enjoyed reading those long and boring texts assigned by your uninspiring teachers. To overcome language barriers, describe things thoroughly. The more specific and accurate your descriptions are, the better the chances the receiver has of interpreting your message the way in which you would like it to be perceived. Increase the accuracy of your messages by using language that describes rather than evaluates by presenting obvious facts, events, and circumstances.

When you have to speak in public, always try to choose words your audience will understand (see chapter 10).

OVERCOMING LISTENING BARRIERS

Most of us simply do not listen well!Perhaps the most common barrier to reception is simply a lack of attention on the receiver's part. Even if we try to concentrate on the words of the sender of a message, we all let our minds wander now and then. Essentially, people are likely to drift off when they are forced to listen to information that is difficult to understand or that has little direct bearing on their own lives.One effective technique to overcome listening barriers is to paraphrase what you have heard and understood.It is very helpful to try to stand in the shoes of the other speakers. It is also important to that urge we all have: jumping to conclusions. Try to get clarification by listening without interrupting the other and asking non-threatening questions. When all of this is done you will understand what the receiver has intended for you to hear. The knowledge you can gain is then limitless.

OVERCOMING EMOTIONAL BARRIERS

Every message contains two meanings: (1) the subject of the message itself; and (2) a relationship meaning, which identifies the most important reason for the interaction between sender and receiver. Communication can break down when the receiver reacts negatively to either of these meanings. You may have to deal with people during emotional times. Either they may be upset, or you might be upset. An angry person is inclined to distort or even ignore the words of the other person. Angry persons are usually incapable of presenting their feelings and ideas in an effective manner. This is not to say that you should avoid all communication when you are emotionally involved, but you should be aware of the potential for misunderstandings that go together with aroused emotions. To overcome emotional barriers during communication, it is important to monitor your own feelings and the feelings of others. Always try to control your negative feelings or anger. Most importantly recognize the probability for misunderstanding that usually goes along with emotional messages.

OVERCOMING BACKGROUND BARRIERS

Each person was raised in a different setting. Along with parents and childhood influences, people are perceived things differently depending on their age, education, gender, social status, economic position, cultural background, temperament, health, beauty, popularity, religion, political beliefs, and so on. People can be influenced greatly by a passing mood.

All of these things can separate one person from another and make communication difficult.

Differences in background are the hardest communication barrier to overcome. To overcome the barriers associated with differing backgrounds, avoid projecting your own background or culture onto others. Clarify your background and understand the background of others. Take into consideration their education, experiences, personalities, perceptions, and do not assume that certain behaviors mean the same thing to everyone.

BECOMING AN EFFECTIVE COMMUNICATOR

In her excellent book, Hamlin (2006) argues that effective communication depends for a large part on what kind of communicator you are. If you are an effective communicator, people would always like to listen to you. There are basically only two types of speakers: appealing speaker and not appealing speakers. The table below will clarify the traits and qualities of appealing speakers.

Warm, friendly, open, honest speakers	A comedian is a great example because they usually put us at ease. The speaker invites us to relax and relate more directly and openly us. Most of us are guarded communicators while these speakers have the great ability to communicate in an unguarded way. It proves how comfortable and secure someone must be to behave this way.
Exciting, creative, interesting speakers	It is truly a pleasure to communicate with these speakers. They have the rare talent of arousing feelings of anticipation and curiosity in others. Their listeners cannot wait for the next thing they want to say.
Knowledgeable, confident speakers	These speakers give reassurance. They are obviously well educated on the subject. We listen and trust our internal instinct that listening will be beneficial
Organized speakers	Our brains need order and logic and these speakers fulfill these needs. The information they provide is delivered in an easily absorbed and recognizable format. We need to see, hear, and picture the structure in the order that underlies the message, especially in today's technological world
Authentic speakers	These speakers are honest about what they want to say. They do not hide the truth. A truthful person speaking from the heart is without deception or hidden agendas
Inspiring speakers	These speakers allow us to follow them. We are carried by their enthusiasm and originality

| Informal speakers | These speakers move right into the comfort zone of casual conversation: no orating, lecturing, or heavy-handed instruction. The message becomes digestible, in bite-sized pieces. Very relaxed |
| Funny speakers | Although being funny is a trait desired by many, not all of us are naturally funny. Genuinely funny speakers are naturally funny and can consistently monitor the appropriateness of their jokes. |

HOW MEN AND WOMEN COMMUNICATE

Research has shown that the communication styles of men and women differ significantly (Liaw, 2005). This difference will help a couple manage their finances more effectively and achieve goals more efficiently. Unfortunately, these advantages are not experienced by all men and women. The compatibility might not arise in daily interactions because both are more consumed by their differences and both do not experience the advantages of cooperation.

Men are more inclined to express their needs, interests, and wants and then wait until others do the same things. Women, in turn, are inclined to ask or end their sentences with a question. This will often lead men to guess what their female partner wants. Women will gently give answers without expressing what they exactly want.

Men talk and interrupt much more whereas women like to react on something said by others and often do not come back to the topic at hand after being interrupted.

Men talk about money in a competitive way: "My investment in the stock market went up." On the other hand women do not talk about money in a competitive way. They even try to avoid the subject of money in their conversations.

Let have a closer look at the different characters of men and women.

Character of Men

Men like to talk about impersonal topics and rarely admit having financial problems and need help to solve them. They are inclined to emphasize the joys of freedom from obligations and make decisions without consulting their partner. Men like to go straight to the point of the problem or do an important thing to achieve their goals. For instance, men go to the toilet to deliver something. On the other hand, women use the toilet to powder their noses, gossip and hang around. Obviously women consider the toilet to be a multifunctional room.

When communicating, men like to start talking about a problem at hand and focus on it whereas women do the opposite. This is caused by the fact that men have a mono-tracking brain causing them to be able to focus on one topic of conversation. When the conversation touches many other topics and drags on, they will stop absorbing relevant information. Women are much better to engage in conversations covering many topics because they havemulti-tracking brains.

How to Communicate with Men

The character of men is stiffer compared to women and this must be understood during conversations. Avoid communication styles which are not to the point. This will not impress them and they will think badly about their counterparts. So try speak to the point, analyze a problem thoroughly, avoid side tracking, use logic when expressing an opinion, avoid talking about other people, use simple words and a firm voice, appreciate them (stimulate their ego), avoid belittling them with negative judgments, and avoid debates if possible. Use exact numbers when talking to men. By using a more rational style emphasizing numbers and figures, men will be able to understand better. So when giving directions, avoid vague markings but give exact signs they can use to find their way.

Character of Women

There are huge differences between the characters of men and women. Women like to talk about themselves, their financial problems, and do not hesitate to ask for help if necessary. They do not consider that to be a burden. Thanks to their multi-tracking brain, women can talk about different topics in a fast way which is an amazing thing. Women like talk about other people. They can talk about others for hours with their female friends. The easily express their feelings and opinions. They value friendship a lot and will ask for help and guidance from their friends. They are less independent in decision making and need the help of men in this respect.

Women like to hear nice words which sound like music in their ears. They discuss sensitive issues indirectly and use imaginary examples to discuss a problem. However, they are good listeners and it is difficult to accuse them of lying. Women are superb in detecting sincerity of others through their body language and tone of voice. For this reason, men like to lie through the phone which is much safer!

How to Communicate with Women

Women with all their beauty are much more sensitive than men and have many other superior traits which all require a gentle approach. When we make a mistake it is going to be difficult to fix it. When communicating with women try to avoid being to the point, talk about social things and daily life to attract their attention, use gentle and civilized words, use social and psychological words, use moderate tone of voice, and use decent and focused body language. It is possible to emphasize some topics, but avoid statistics, numbers and other exact data. Use a warm and friendly psychological approach. Appreciate them by praising all women in general. Of course compliment their clothes and accessories at the start of conversation. Women like to form friendships instead of cold and stiff business relationships. They like to foster long-term relationships and unlike men, they do not like to look at relationships with a cost-benefit approach. When giving directions do it like this: "The address you are looking for is nor far from here. You just need to pass McDonald's on your left and the building you are looking for is just in front of you." There are no exact numbers in this explanation and this will be much better understood by women than men.

HIPPOCRATES PERSONALITY QUARTET AS A COMMUNICATION TOOL

A lot of people probably have purchased one of the books written by the famous couple Florence and Fred Littauer. They discussed an ancient old personality quartet or four basic types of personality all humans seem to have. Why is it ancient old? It was actually the famous Greek physician Hippocrates who lived from 460 until 377 B.C. who introduced the four human 'temperaments': choleric, sanguine, phlegmatic, and melancholic. The famous Russian physiologist Pavlov has also used and refined the Hippocratic scheme. The Littauers, however, have made the quartet available for a wide audience because they have been able to make a practical tool. Their most important advice is: know yourself first before you can know someone else. The four personality types, as emphasized by Hippocrates and repeated by the Littauers, cannot be considered to be completely separate and distinct from each other. In reality, most persons represent 'in-between' types.

The choleric

What are actually the typical characteristics of these four personality types? The *choleric* emotions are very easily triggered because this person is highly excitable. The *Choleric* is show a lot of passion in their actions and their speech. Their movements tend to be quick and swift. He/she is bold and ambitious but tends to be reckless. They do not necessarily think before they speak. Sometimes this gets the *choleric* into trouble. The best way to communicate with this personality type is by using clear and precise words, systematic explanations, and by avoiding words like 'maybe', 'perhaps' or any other words which might arouse feelings of uncertainty. It makes sense not to engage in debates with these people if you do not have certain facts which can be used to counter them. Instead of debating with them, it is better to let them expose their thoughts in a clear manner and praise the *choleric* for what they have said without overdoing it.

The melancholic

The *melancholic,* in turn, can be seen as the opposite of the choleric because this person is considered to be reserved.The melancholic person is perceived by others as slowly thinking and somewhat depressed. As an introvert, the melancholic has difficulty making friends, but he/she is reliable because of their dependability and determination. These are their strong traits. The best way to communicate with the melancholic type is by using facts and other objective data. Limit too much humor, do not show boredom and avoid excessive use of motivational words.When communicating with these people, give them the opportunity to express their thoughts completely because they need enough time to think before giving answers.

The phlegmatic

The in-between groups consist of the sanguine and phlegmatic types. The *sanguine* have a tendency towards excitement, while the *phlegmatic* have a tendency towards inhibition. The phlegmatic person is stable and calm. He/she may even look cool, sluggish or even uninterested. Normally quiet and reserved, he/she does not easily befriend others. The best way to communicate with the phlegmatic type is by using a soft voice when talking, explain your thoughts in a slow manner, being consistent in what you say and do, avoid topics which might cause conflicts, and emphasizing the decisions made. Phlegmatic's tend to accommodate themselves with many different things. Always give them time to think about what you said by allowing them to be silent.

The sanguine

The *sanguine* person is stable, yet active. He/she is courageous, hopeful, passionate and cheerful, but somewhat inconstant. He/she is courteous, lively, alert, and demonstrative. The best way to communicate with the sanguine type is to speak with enthusiasm, use a lot of motivational words, be positive and energetic all the time, be complementary, and use visual aids and illustrations when explaining something. Never debate about minor details with these persons and always show energetic body language.

The following table summarizes the communication styles of the Hippocrates personality quartet:

Hippocrates Personality Type	Best Way To Communicate
Choleric	Using clear and precise words, systematic explanations, avoid words like 'maybe' and 'perhaps.' Avoid debating with them without facts. Let them expose their thoughts in a clear manner. Volunteer praise, but do not go overboard with it.
Melancholic	Strong and concise. Use facts and other recognizable information, limit humor, avoid showing boredom and excessive use of motivational words. Give these people time to think before expecting answers. Let them express themselves thoroughly without pushing them forward.
Sanguine	Be positive, energetic, and complementary. Speak with enthusiasm, use many motivational words. Avoid debating about minor details with these persons. Use visual aids such as illustrations when explaining something. Show interest by using energetic body language.
Phlegmatic	Avoid topics which might cause conflicts. Use a low, soft voice and explain your thoughts slowly and be consistent in what you say and do. Give emphasis to the decisions made because they tend to commit themselves to many promises. Always give them time to think about what you said by allowing them to be silent.

If one does not know a person very well, Hippocrates personality quartet can certainly be used as an effective tool during interactions. Communicating will then become easier if you know what you are and what the other person may be. However, personality is a 'tricky' thing with many limitations. There are actually many personality typologies available. The Myers-Briggs Type Indicator offers sixteen different personalities and how can we know which personality fits us or another person? It will take a lot of memorizing and analysis before that is known. An interesting typology is called the *Enneagram* which divides all people into nine basic personalities (Goldberg, 1997).

THE ENNEGRAM PERSONALITY TYPES

The Perfectionist

These are people with a need to get things right. Perfectionists are usually critical, idealistic, and judgmental. Decisions are made with an internalized 'single correct way' in mind. Their work is meant to reflect extremely high standards set by themselves. Continually, they are teaching, preaching, and monitoring others. This causes others to feel nit-picked or rejected. Perfectionist fiercest anger is directed toward themselves. At their best, Perfectionists are honest, idealistic, visionaries. They have a clear vision of what should be, with the ability to direct others.

The Helper

Helpers strive to be appreciated. They give with the intention of reciprocal gratitude. Helpers are relationship oriented with an emotionally seductive attitude. Sweet and manipulative, helpers make themselves indispensable to and adored by others. This is their path to influence and seek power. Helpers have impeccable radar for others feeling, preferences, and appetites. They excel in customer services, are genuinely sensitive, and humble. Helpers serve and bring out the best in others.

The Producer

Producers are more than likely workaholics. They enjoy being applauded for getting the job done. Producers can be high performing, enthusiastic, and competitive. It is essential that they be rewarded for their achievements. Some might say that Producers are self involved and obsessed with image. They come off as insensitive, superficial, artificial and expedient. Producers are often seen merely as their resume. At their best Producers are eager, efficient leaders with the ability to problem solve and influence others.

The Connoisseur

It is easy for a Connoisseur to gravitate toward the beautiful, authentic, true and unusual. These people are romantic and melancholic. Connoisseurs manifest impeccable taste within their concerns. They look for deeper meaning underneath the surface. Feelings are what drive their decisions. Connoisseurs seem to be satisfied with the impeccable. They can seem intense or snooty. At their best they are creative and imaginable. Connoisseurs love the attractiveness, taste, and elegance in the world.

The Sage

Sages seek mastery over their personal domains. They are emotionally detached. It is said that sages observe the world from safe vantage points. Here they can stockpile facts, theories, and information. Sages do not rely on relationships but instead camouflage themselves and minimize needs. Others see them as emotionally detached, as they hide behind whatever they can find. At best, Sages are sensitive, brilliant, respectful, intense, entrepreneurs. Committed and most wizards in their fields.

The Troubleshooter

Paranoid at best, troubleshooters are preoccupied with worse case scenarios. Trust is a huge issue. They are over prepared and obsessed with what could possibly go wrong. Others may find their procrastination frustrating. Troubleshooters can be faithful, imaginative, original thinkers, intuitive, committed, sensitive, and courageous. They are known for defending their team, their boss, and themselves. Troubleshooters are terrific at pointing out pitfalls and hidden motives along the way.

The Visionary

Visionaries stay positive and keep all options open. They engage, plan, and have high energy romances. Visionaries have difficulty growing up. They are known as superficial Peter Pans. It is not easy for visionaries to consider pitfalls. Therefore, they avoid completion, pain, conflict, ordinary commitments, and routine work. Although they initiate progress they often times neglect to follow through. The best Visionaries are gifted, witty, inspirational, and charming. Their ideas and enthusiasm pull people toward them.

The Top Dog

Power and control are what Top Dogs seek. They express their feelings freely and loudly. Top Dogs are described to be domineering and blunt. They loudly seek out confrontations believing the truth often comes out in a fight. They focus on their own powers and others shortcomings. Others may be repelled by their flamboyant bullying. At best Top Dogs are nurturing of the underdogs with whom they are in charge of.

The Mediator

Mediators seek to include all people and all points of view. These people compromise easily. They can see the feelings, needs, and enthusiasms of others. Others may see Mediators as neglectful or spacey. At their best, mediators lead by inspiring others. They are warm and openhearted individuals. Mediators are naturally in touch with the flow of the group. Therefore, mediators are excellent diplomats, team builders, and boundary spanners.

The following table summarizes the communication styles of the nine *Enneagram* personality styles:

Enneagram Personality Type	**Best Way to Communicate**
Perfectionist	Follow their instructions. Recognize their accomplishments. Confirm their past deeds. Always say that you appreciate their advice. Be honest and offer them full attention. Say sorry when you forget or negligent. Gently stimulate them to be happy.

Helper
Always say you appreciate them. Be happy with them. Be interested in their problems. Say that they are important and unique. Be diplomatic when criticizing them.

Producer
Leave them alone when they are working. Give honest critique, judgment, or feedback. Emphasize harmony and peace. Avoid projecting negative feelings. Always say that you like to be near them. Say you are proud of them..

Connoisseur
Give a lot of praises; it means a lot to them. Be a supportive friend. Help them love themselves. Praise their intuition and vision. Help them overcome worries. Avoid telling them of being oversensitive

Sage
Speak honestly, directly, and be brief. Avoid being too close with them. They need time to be alone and think. Avoid communicating like a bulldozer. Help them avoid irritations: big parties, hard music, high emotions, and intrusion of their privacy.

Troubleshooter
Be direct and clear. Listen attentively. Do not judge their fears. Work together with them until the job is done. Persuade them that everything is ok between the two of you. Laugh and make jokes. Gently persuade them gain new experiences.

Visionary
Give them friendship, love, and freedom. Engage in entertaining conversation and laugh with them. Listen to their dreams. Avoid changing them. Avoid questioning what they are doing.

Top Dog
Defend your opinions: they do not like 'weak' people. Avoid gossiping about them and betray their trust in you. Be open and acknowledge their character. Accept it when they yell because that is their nature.

Mediator
Listen to what they say even if it is not interesting. Ask questions so that they can explain clearly. Always praise them. Seek discussions, but avoid confrontations. Laugh with them and enjoy life with them.

The *Enneagram* is actually similar to the personality typology offered by numerology. The only difference is that personality number five and seven are switched.

Aside from these typologies available in the market, the most important question which must be answered is: how can we use our personality effectively? If we can use our personality more effectively, we will become better communicators and perhaps even get more success in life. Much has been written about improving our personalities and the message is always positive: you can always become what you want. Of course one cannot change everything in one's self, but attempts can be undertaken to improve our self-image and communication performance.

HOW TO IMPROVE YOUR PERSONALITY

Usually the advice given in many written texts and repeated over and over again by numerous communication *gurus* can be summarized in the following points (Dudley, 1996):

1. *Concentrate on one thing at a time.* Many people who plans to improve their personality feel that they need to boost their confidence. Confidence is the most important building block of success in almost all human activities. However, personality is a complex mixture of habits, physical, mental and emotional. The challenge of improving personality will require it to be broken down into certain specific habits which require development. Improvement is a slow process. Each obstacle has to be tackled separately. In the end, cultivating confidence will boost self-improvement of other personality traits.

2. *Understand how you came to be what you are.* Try to analyze your own motives. Many of our troubles are caused by our childhood experiences and looking back at them will help us discover the causes. Do not be afraid to look at these original memories. Use your mature adult brain to reevaluate them. The technique you need to apply is going over each experience in your mind repetitively. Slowly and consistently try to work off the emotions connected with them. Only stop when you can think about those experiences without becoming upset again.

3. *Imagine yourself becoming what you want be.* Many people think that lack of confidence can be resolved through an effort of will. The best way is actually a combination of will-power and the power of imagination. Imagination and will together are more effective together than separately. Try to picture yourself in your mind as the person you would like to be. Imagine a mental picture of yourself and then imagine yourself as a changed person. You can then use your will-power to make the mental picture a reality.

4. *Suggest to yourself that you can be what you imagine.* Stand in front of the mirror and repeatedly tell yourself that you can become what you want to be. Suggest to yourself that you will no longer be afraid of the memories of your past. Continuously confirm to yourself, quietly but forcefully, whatever change you desire. In other words, you can replace fear with confidence. All of this with the help of autosuggestion.

5. *Act the part you want to play in life.* Putting people at ease is actually a simple endeavor. Just show interest in them as you expect them to be interested in you. Show

real and not a fake interest in other people and prove it by talking about the things that interest them. Do not be jealous of the good fortune of others. Show appreciation of others. Speak well of people. Avoid making them feel substandard. Eliminate disapproval and unfavorable criticism. Make a habit to show a friendly smile. Nurture a sense of humor. Listen with sympathy and interest to what others have to say.

This list is not exhaustive because in the end it boils down to our ability to improve our own lives. Communication is of course an important skill in our attempts to improve our lives.

In communication, we need to constantly seek ways to improve our interpersonal communication skills. The way we convey our messages to others must be refined all the time. A very important element in acquiring good communication skills is self-confidence. You need to ask many questions to yourself: do you remain cool in emergencies? Do you avoid blaming others when things go wrong? Can you always be depended upon to do what you say you will do? Do you go out of your way cheerfully to help others? Do you have reasonable faith in humanity? Do you show an interest in the interests of others? Do you take an active part in any organizations in which you belong?

Another element which is related to the above issue is our ability to imagine ourselves becoming what we want to be. The power of visualization or imagination is extremely important if you want to change yourself or at least become a better communicator. The combination of will and imagination is very strong and will help you change in a positive way. If you want to change yourself, but your imagination dwells on thoughts of failure, then you will fail. This is called the law of reversed effort.

Finally, you need to be able to talk yourself into change. This technique is called affirmation. You should constantly repeat to yourself what you want to change. If you want to become a better communicator, you should repeatedly say to yourself: I am a good communicator! Avoid saying: I will become a good communicator because you might fail. You must picture yourself as already a person who is a superb communicator!

TEN COMMANDMENTS OF INTERCULTURAL COMMUNICATION

The lines of business which were once clearly marked are now more of a blur. Lately, companies around the world are hopping national borders to conduct business on a regular basis. Do not be surprised that some day you will join an organization where you will met and work with people coming from different national, religious, and ethnic backgrounds. Communicating across language and cultural barriers can be a difficult task. Thanks to globalization you do not have to leave your own country in order to come into contact with people from a variety of backgrounds. These people with different backgrounds will work within your company, industry, and community.

Communicating with people from other cultures can be challenging. However, your success in business and career will be determined by your ability to communicate effectively with people coming from different cultures. To overcome cultural barriers, there has to be a means of effective communication. First, you must learn what culture actually means. *Culture is a shared system of symbols, beliefs, attitudes, values, expectations, and norms for behavior. Subcultures, in turn, are distinct groups that exist within a major culture.*

Cultures differ in several ways that affect communication:

- *Stability:* cultures do not necessarily stay the same. Conditions in the culture may be stable or may be changing either slowly or rapidly.

- *Complexity:* the accessibility of information varies throughout different cultures.

- *Composition:* many cultures are made up of many diverse subcultures. You can expect to communicate easier with persons with fewer subcultures in their background because there are fewer potential differences to consider.

- *Acceptance:* cultures vary in their attitudes toward outsiders. Some cultures are openly hostile, while others are friendly. Some cultures show a detached aloofness: they do not care about outsiders. These factors will determine the level of trust and effective communication you can achieve with people of other cultures.

The following table provides a more detailed specification of Asian and Western values

Asian values	Western values
Collectivism	Individualism
Harmonious relationships	Self-actualization
Hierarchies and power distance	Democratic
Low tolerance of uncertainty/risk	Tolerance of uncertainty/risk
Respect for elders	Respect for merit
Respect for status	Respect for achievement
Face, sensitivity and feelings	Objective facts and data
Indirect; third party assistance	Direct to the point; one to

one	
Shame culture – external control	Guilt culture – internal control
Modesty and humility	Winning, assertive, active and outspoken
Guarded; limited disclosure	More disclosure
Consensus seeking	Consultative; debate
Collaboration	Competitiveness
Personal and group face	Personal pride and self-esteem
Relationship focused	Task focused
Family spirit; unity	Role and boundary definition
Time is life	Time is money
Being	Doing
Humanistic and spiritual fulfillment	Mechanistic and materialistic

Source: Burns, 1998

By bridging these differences, you can successfully achieve effective intercultural communication. However, the four elements of culture are very general in nature. They do not say much about how to communicate with persons from other cultures.

TEN COMMANDMENTS OF INTERCULTURAL COMMUNICATION

1. **Watch for different social values.** As a general consensus, people in many western countries assume that people from other cultures also disapprove of poverty and value hard work. In fact, many societies condemn materialism, while others tolerate a more carefree lifestyle.

2. **Watch for different roles and status symbols and how to demonstrate them.** Culture determines the roles people play. Culture determines who communicates with whom, what is being communicated, and in the ways of communication. In many countries, women do not play a prominent role in business. Consequently, female executives who visit these countries may find that they are not taken serious in business dealings. Another difference is concepts of status. It is common in many Western countries to see executives use certain status signals to reflect materialistic values. In the West, a big boss has a large corner office, deep carpets, an expensive desk, and handsome accessories. However, in the Middle East, fine possessions can be found in private homes while business is conducted in modest and often cramped quarters.

3. **Watch for decision making customs**. Western people like to make decisions quickly and efficiently. The opposite customs can be found in Greece. A Greek executive perceives a person who ignores the details as being evasive and untrustworthy. This goes to show you that research is necessary before attempting a business transaction in a country other than your own.

4. **Watch for concepts of time**. In many western countries, time is money. In the perception of many Westerners, time is used to plan the business day efficiently. All tasks will be executed in a separate scheduled time. In many Latin American and Asian countries, meeting deadlines is not as important as building a good long-term business relationship.

5. **Watch for personal space**. Do not assume that the 'comfort zone' in your own culture is the same as in other cultures. Canadian and US business persons would like to have a comfortable conversation by standing about five feet apart. An uncomfortably close distance for people from Germany or Japan. Arabs or Latin Americans will consider this distance as uncomfortably far.

6. **Watch for cultural context**. People from the USA (called 'low-context cultures') rely heavily on verbal communication. Implied meaning and circumstances are considered unimportant. People from South Korea and Taiwan ('high-context cultures') rely less on verbal communication and more on the context of nonverbal actions and environmental settings to convey meaning.

7. **Watch for body language**. All different cultures have different body languages. People in the United States and Canada show agreement by shaking their heads back and forth.; people in Bulgaria nod up and down; people in Japan move their right hands; people in Sicily raise their chins. Show your awareness by using the correct body language and this can only be done after you have learned the basic differences in the way people supplement their words with body language.

8. **Watch for different etiquette; rules or manners**. What is perceived to be polite in one culture may be perceived to be rude in another culture. For example, in Arab countries it is improper to offer gifts to a man's wife. The proper way is to offer his children gifts. These cultural rules should be studied before attempting a meeting.

9. **Watch for legal and ethical behavior**. In some countries, government officials expect to receive extra fees from various companies before they approve government contracts. These payments are not illegal or unethical; they are simply routine aspects of life. However, the same payments are seen as bribes in the United States, Sweden, and many other countries. These payments are considered illegal and unethical.

10. **Watch for language barriers**. Although English is the most used language in international business, you cannot assume that everyone speaks it. When you deal with people who do not speak your language at all, you have options. Some of which include: learning their language, using an intermediary or translator, or teach them English. All have to be well thought out and or researched in advance.

Learning as much as possible about another culture will facilitate your chances to communicate effectively with its members. Your abilities will be noticed if you read books and articles about the culture, and talk to people who have done business with the members of that particular culture. Concentrate on learning something about the culture's history, religion, politics, values, and customs. Try to find out what the subcultures, business subculture, and rules of protocol are valid in a certain country.

- *Take responsibility for communication.* You are always responsible for the communication and you cannot assume that it is the other person's responsibility to communicate with you.

- *Withhold judgments.* Learn to listen to the entire story while accepting differences in others without judging them.

- *Show respect.* Learn how respect is communicated. Do your research as to what gestures, eye contact, and other nonverbal cues are used in various cultures.

- *Empathize.* Try to understand the other person's feelings and point of view; be sensitive to what he or she is trying to communicate and why.

- *Tolerate ambiguity.* Many people will become frustrated when placed in an unfamiliar or confusing situation. It is important to control your frustration in intercultural communication settings.

- *Look beyond the superficial.* Do not be distracted by such things as dress, appearance or environmental discomforts. Show your ability to adapt accordingly.

- *Be patient and persistent.* Do not give up easily when communicating with someone from another culture. Continue to try to get your own point across until it is fully understood.

- *Recognize your own cultural biases.* Try to identify your own assumptions and how they are different from the other person's.

- *Be flexible.* Communicating with someone from another culture will force you to change your habits and attitudes. This is a sign of respect for the other person and their culture.

- *Emphasize common ground.* Look for similarities; this will give you a common ground to work from.

- *Send clear messages.* Try to send clear and consistent verbal as well as nonverbal signals.

- *Increase your cultural sensitivity.* A lot of miscommunication can be avoided if you are willing to learn more about variations in customs and practices.

- *Deal with the individual.* Many people make the mistake of stereotyping the other person who then becomes a representative a certain group while this might not be true. Try to communicate with each person as an individual, not as a member of another group.

- *Learn when to be direct.* Being direct is not always appreciated in many cultures. Investigate when you can send your message directly or and when to send it indirectly.

How to Communicate in the Workplace

Humans are unique in terms of behavior. They show all kinds of different behavior even if they are confronted with the same situations. This is especially true in the workplace. Some workers like to constantly do something in order to get things done and have a feeling of accomplishment. Others like influence others to get things done whereas others try to connect people in order to accomplish something. These three characters can be identified as *doers, influencers, and connectors* (Liaw, 2005). These three characters have become important figures in the new world of work which is nowadays called the knowledge economy. The doers, influencers, and connectors are basically the new knowledge workers.

How to communicate with *doers*

These people like to act fast in order to get things done fast. They are inclined go straight to the heart of the problem without any formalities. They try to avoid all kinds of minor details and try to find the best short cuts otherwise they will face boredom. They cherish freedom and accept its risks. They are innovators who often start their own business. They like being acknowledged by the public for their achievements in their area of expertise. They do not like theories and discourses; they like to act. These doers can be found most often in the world of business. They do what they need to do without consulting management textbooks. They are just interested in one thing: action.

They do not like small talk because they want to be to the point. When communicating with doers also try to be straight to the point, avoid complicated stories, speak in direct and short sentences, give direct responses, and avoid theories and debating about their views. In short, try to deliver your messages in a straightforward manner and avoid complicated facts which are difficult to comprehend with common sense. Always appreciate their actions and give fast responses to avoid their boredom.

How to communicate with *influencers*

These persons like to process their thoughts in a verbal manner. They like to 'think hard' when communicating with others. They like to interrupt others especially if the topic of discussion. They do not consider it to be an interruption, but as part of a lively conversation. They like to interact with others because they are polite, creative, and persuasive. However, they need someone else to do their job. They like social interactions, recognition, and opportunities to show off their creativity. They like to help others solve a problem because they are good in forming long lasting relationships. They like others with sincerity, but this might lead to sad dramas because they do not realize the psychological impacts of their interventions in other people's lives. Their most favorite activity in their spare time is teasing others.

When communicating with the influencer use cheerful words because they like happiness, allow them to cut off your sentence as long as the conversation is continued afterwards, show sympathy when they are talking, pretend to be influenced by them, and avoid debating with them. If you control yourself, these people will not be able to influence you. Ironically, they are truly impressed by others who are not influenced by them.

How to communicate with *connectors*

These persons are the connectors of several persons who are experiencing a common problem. They are hard workers and trustworthy persons. They like to listen to opinions of others than giving their own opinions. Although they seem to be tough at times, they can accept changes as long as they are useful for themselves and others. When communication with connectors try to be honest and to the point, ask what they have done so far, praise them in a personal and sincere way, appreciate them with smiles and other relevant body language to show your admiration for them, always say that they know better, avoid small talk, and ask for their opinions and praise their opinions. Connectors are effective workers who can follow instructions well if you know how to appreciate their accomplishments. They will become good colleagues if we can speak with in a straightforward and responsible manner. Consistency is also important for them and it will all lead to the fulfillment of expected outcomes.

GOOD COMMUNICATORS MANAGE THEIR BODY LANGUAGE

Nonverbal communication is usually unplanned, but it has a much bigger impact than verbal communication. Researchers have discovered that nonverbal cues account for 93 percent of the emotional meaning that is exchanged in any interaction. Nonverbal cues play an important role in conveying feelings. Of course all messages will reflect the blending of nonverbal and verbal communication. Mood-altering chemicals will be releases in the sender and the receiver thanks to nonverbal communication. Smiling will always make us feel happier. Guarded gestures, in turn, will only stimulate our hostility and limit our receptivity.

Nonverbal communication is extremely powerful because it is always reliable. For many persons, deceiving others with words is far easier than with their bodies. A lot of persons can control their words, but have less control over their body language, facial expressions, and vocal characteristics. Whether a speaker is honest or not can best be discovered by observing these nonverbal cues. For this reason, we all tend to put more faith in nonverbal cues. We automatically believe the nonverbal signals of others when their verbal and nonverbal signals conflict with each other. The credibility of an individual as a communicator will to a great degree depend on nonverbal messages.

Nonverbal communication's importance stretches beyond its reliability You can transmit a nonverbal message without even thinking about it and your audience can register the meaning unconsciously. When you have a conscious message, you can often achieve it more reasonably with a gesture than with words. Waves of the hand, a pat on the back, a wink – all are streamlined expressions of thought. . It can be effective from both the sender's and receiver's standpoint. Although nonverbal communication can stand alone, it is usually mixed with speech, covering part of the message. Together, the two modes of expression are a powerful combination augmenting, reinforcing, and clarifying one another.

There are over 700,000 forms of nonverbal communication which can be grouped into the following categories: facial expressions and eye behavior, gestures and postures, vocal characteristics, personal appearance, touching behavior, and lastly, use of time and space. Certain nonverbal signals reflect certain distinct meanings. However, it is the observer who determines the meaning of nonverbal communication because he or she will be able to read the specific signals and interpret them in the context of a particular situation.

Facial Expressions and Eye Behavior

Your face is the primary place for expressing your emotions. Your face will reveal the type and the intensity of your feelings. Your eyes will reveal your attention and interest, capability of influencing others, regulating interaction, and establishing dominance. In the West, eye contact is extremely important: your audience might perceive your positive message to be a negative one because you have averted your gaze. People often manipulate their expressions to show an emotion they do not feel and or to mask their true feelings; then the eyes and the face will become unreliable sources of meaning.

Gestures and Postures

You can expose specific and general messages by moving your body: some voluntary and some involuntary. Many gestures like a wave of the hand have a specific and intentional meaning, such as "hello" or "goodbye." Other types of gestures are unintentional and expose a more general message. Confidence or the opposite feeling of nervousness is usually demonstrated by slouching, learning forward, fidgeting, and walking briskly. The same can be said about demonstrating gestures which reflects friendliness or hostility, assertiveness or passivity, powerfulness or powerlessness. Be careful that your body movement is not reflecting an incorrect view of your thoughts and or attitude.

Vocal Characteristics.

Your voice reflects intentional and unintentional messages. Mindfully, we can use our voices to create a variety of impressions. Consider the sentence "How are you?" If you repeat that question four or five times, changing your tone of voice and stressing an assortment of words, several different messages can be sent. However, your vocal characteristics also reveal many things that you are unaware of. Your tone and volume of voice, your accent, and speaking pace will reveal a lot about who you are, your relationship with the audience, and the emotions underlying your words.

Personal appearance.

Your appearance helps establish your social identity. Unfortunately, people respond to us on the basis of our physical attractiveness. This is because we see ourselves as others see us. We are ranked on the basis of our physical attractiveness. We will feel good about ourselves when people think we are attractive and capable. And this will affect our behavior which will then affect other people's perceptions of us. These expectations will often become a selffulfilling prophecy. Despite the limits of altering body type and facial features, most of us can, to some degree, control our attractiveness. Our grooming, clothing, accessories, and style have a large impact on our appearance. If you want to make a good impression, simply imitate the style of the people you want to impress.

Touching behavior.

Touch is a very effective way to convey warmth, comfort, and reassurance. The most casual contact can create positive feelings because it suggests intimacy. However, touching is regulated by relatively strict customs that determines who can touch whom, where, and how. The accepted norms depend on gender, age, relative status, and cultural background of the persons involved. Touching in especially office settings has become controversial because it can sometimes be interpreted as sexual harassment.

Use of time and space.

Time and space can be used to enforce authority. In many Eastern cultures, people demonstrate their importance by making other people wait. People can also demonstrate their status by occupying different amounts of space. Space can determine how comfortable people feel when communicating with each other. We will feel at ease when people stand not too close or too far away. However, culture has a big impact on attitudes related to punctuality, comfort zones, and other nonverbal communication elements.

Ten Positive Body Language Habits of Highly Effective Communicators:

1. **Show that you are really listening by nodding thoughtfully.** Communication will become extremely effective when we center our attention on the speaker. The speaker will then be able to give good information and our ability to hear him or her will also improve.

2. **Show interest in the other person by orienting your body towards the other person.** The speaker will feel encouraged to continue if you orient your body towards him or her.   If the communication is important, focus entirely on the speaker and what he or she is saying. Try to push any other thoughts from your mind because this will avoid you from becoming distracted by other things that might be going on around you.

3. **Show openness by pointing your feet towards the other person.** If a person's feet are pointed away from you, it can be interpreted as a negative signal. Something is then missing in the communication process. Pointing your feet toward the other person shows that you are listening and appreciating the message which is being conveyed.

4. **Be positive by stroking your chin.** This can be interpreted as a positive signal. The other person approves or agrees with what you are saying. They are interested in what is being said.

5. **Show attention through eye contact.** Eye contact is another aspect which can be interpreted as a positive signal. When the other person appreciates the way you are communicating, his or her pupils will be dilated or enlarged.

6. **Show constructive attitude by a relaxed posture.** If the other person has crossed arms all the time during a conversation, then you know that person is a closed person or closes him/herself from you. This conveys that they are uncomfortable, or they disagree with what is being said. They are closing themselves off in disagreement.

7. **Show openness by keeping your hands open.** When the other person is sending a negative signal, he or she might show that by forming a fist or clenching hands. In turn, tightly clenched hands might be a sign of frustration. Drumming fingers is undoubtedly a sign of boredom. Open hands reflects a positive interpretation of the communication process.

8. **Show that you are focused by thoughtful 'um-hums.'** These are always perceived as positive signals in any communication settings. However, rapidly exchanging breaths is clearly a negative signal. Deep breaths reflect boredom and short breaths reflects frustration.

9. **Show co-operation by an open body position.** Openness of thoughts, mind, and attitudes are usually signaled by open gestures and body position. An open body position can reveal trust towards the other because you open yourself to communication. You show that you are willing to hear what others are saying.

Show willingness to solve something by handling documents or materials presented to you. If documents or materials presented are not handled promptly, this might be interpreted as unwillingness to solve something urgent. Setting aside documents or materials presented might be seen as a negative reaction to the situation. Instead, show respect by paying close attention to what is being handed to you. Once you have gone over the documents you can then decide in which order the work should proceed.

How to communicate with expressers, drivers, and analyzers

People express themselves in different ways because they have different characters. Some like to express themselves with a lot of joy whereas as others like to drive others to do something while others again like to use their analytical minds to analyze something. From this short introduction it is clear that there are at least three types of people who use different ways to express themselves: expressers, drivers, and analyzers (Liaw, 2005).

How to communicate with *expressers*

These people are always in joyful mood and like to ask about others. They like to know what others are doing and not what the outcome will be. They do not like complicated explanations to avoid losing the happy moments they have. They are truly social beings because they enjoy social life, mingling, interacting, and joking with everyone they meet. They hate dry facts which only cause stress and will reduce their happiness. They are more inclined to do 'fun' things. They are straight forward and to the point. They do not like poems and old songs full with flowery words. They like things to be brief and clear. When communicating with expressers try to follow their happy rhythm, show the same joy as they do, clap your hands if necessary, avoid competing with them, give enthusiastic responses, acknowledge their professional achievements, react fast to their messages, and give them challenges which they will surely like. Always try to be happy when communication wit them. They are simple people who dislike complicated things. By following their style a harmonious relationship can be formed with them.

How to communicate with *drivers*

These kind of people have a high drive to stimulate others do things as they want them to be. It is important to stay in control otherwise you might really be doing only what they want. The best way to communicate with them is by letting them lead the beginning and end of the conversation. Let them explain in which direction they want to lead the conversation and let them decide what is best. Praise them gently and expose your message in between your praises. Show accommodative body language through shaking their hands and repeated nodding. These people have bigger egos than the average person and they feel that they are born to lead and drive others. For this reason they are highly self confident and it is important to avoid hurting their egos. If this happens you will not be able to repair this damage. Always follow them and give your messages in a smart way.

How to communicate with *analyzers*

These people have a strong analytic mind and use their left hemisphere of their brain in a very effective way. They are logical and rational thinkers when analyzing a problem. They hate irrationality and unproven methods. When communicating with them it is necessary to have the right data and facts in order to provide correct and valid information. Talk about processes and not results and give them freedom to make decisions. Do not blame them because they do not see themselves as making any mistakes. They are actually poor communicators because they are stiff and hate being criticized. Facts and data will be everything for them and using them will make communicating with them an easy thing. Avoid using to many words when talking to them because they consider you to be wasting their valuable time. The best way to communicate with them is to relax, provide a lot of facts and data and let them decide what is best based on those facts.

IMPROVING EFFECTIVE COMMUNICATION

The word communication originates from the Latin word "cum" which means "with" and it is combined with the word "unus" which means "one". The combination of these two words results in the word "communio" which is translated as "communion" in the English language. Communion can be defined as togetherness and the verb "communicare" has been derived which means sharing something with someone and this word became "communicatio" which is better known as communication.

Communication starts with an idea in the mind of a person. This idea is then processed into a message and sent through a certain medium to someone else. The receiver the message, try to understand it and gives a response to the sender of the message. By receiving the response, the sender can determine whether the original message was understood especially by the person to which the message was directed. Communication is not merely an exchange of words, but it is actually an exchange of meaning of those words. Due to its interactive nature, communication can be seen as a dynamic process. The exchange of meaning makes communication unique which cannot be repeated in exactly the same manner because the situation and the mood of those involved will have changed. For this reason, the impact of communication cannot be changed afterwards; those involved can only change the words, but not the initial impact of the words used previously.

Types of communication

There are several types of communication depending on the objective:

1. *Verbal, written, and electronic communication.* Verbal communication happens with words which are exchanged between at least two persons in a conversation. Through verbal communication, people express their feelings, emotions, thoughts, ideas, meaning, facts, data, and information. Language plays an important role in verbal communication. Written communication can take the form of a letter, memo, report, hand out, flyer, notes, posters, drawings, graphs, etc. The advantages of written communication are that there will be a record of what has been said unlike verbal communication which is usually unrecorded. In addition, there will be more time available to study the content of the written communication at hand. Electronic communication, in turn, takes the form of emails, radio messages, television programs, and facsimiles. The advantages of electronic communication are its high speed and data storage. Messages can be sent through several different media which can be combined. For this reason, electronic communication can be received by several of our senses.

2. *Verbal and non-verbal communication.* Verbal communication cannot take place without language. At first, human communicated with non-verbal language or cues and other physical movements which are called body language. However, as humans evolved, body language was considered inadequate which made way for the development of language. First language was used verbally and later written language developed and nowadays verbal communication also occurs electronically. Verbal language is continuously developing and adjusted to fulfill the needs of changing human beings. For this reason, language is dynamic.

3. *Formal and informal communication.* Formal communication is used in formal institutions. It is a type of communication used in line with formal instructions given by formal figures of authority in accordance with the valid channels and organizational structure. Formal communication is useful for the exchange of messages related to the functioning and performance of formal organizations. Informal communication also occurs in organizations, but is not directed to fulfill the administrative needs of the organization. Informal communication fulfills the social needs of the members of an organization. Informal communication in organizations can also be called the exchange of information in the so-called grapevine.

4. *Intrapersonal communication or communication within oneself.* Unlike animals, human have the ability to think, invent, discover, and explore. These abilities would not be possible without the evolution of a larger brain which needed thousands of years. This ability to communicate intrapresonally is what makes human beings superior to animals. For this reason humans have become the dominant species on the planet.

5. *Interpersonal communication or communication between two persons.* Interpersonal communication can simply be described as face-to-face interaction between tow or more persons in which the sender can send a message directly and receiver of the message can also give a response in a direct way.

6. *Small-group communication.* Individuals choose whether to enter a group or to stay in a group on the basis of which action provides them with the most desirable outcome. Group formation communication can take several forms depending on the structure and size of the group in question.

7. *Mass-communication.* Mass-communication can be distinguished from other kinds of communication by the fact that it is addresses to a large cross-section of a population rather than only one or a few individuals or a special part of the population. The technical means of transmitting the communication are such that the communication may reach at the same time all the people forming the cross-section of the population.

Function of communication

The following can be seen as the functions of communication:

1. Communication in the personal lives of individuals consisting of expressing of feelings, opinions, thoughts, attitude, behavior, emotions, desires, ambitions, and wants.

2. Interpersonal communication to know one another, to become friends, to discuss problems, to exchange thoughts (ideas), to make plans, to get and give help, to mutually help each other change attitudes and behavior.

3. Workplace communication is necessary for getting along with each other at work, create synergy with co-workers, give and receive instructions, and to overcome differences, tensions, and conflicts.

4. Societal communication is necessary to unite the people, overcome societal problems, create societal progress, and produce welfare for everyone.

5. The essential function of communication is to build constructive relationships between persons. In other words, communication has become the most powerful tool to build any relationship between persons. Through communication we can know others and we can become known by others. Communicating translates into disclosing our thoughts, feelings, ideas, and wants to others so that our existence is known to others.

Effective communication

Effective communication has become the ideal of all people who attempt to communicate with each other. Communication will become effective when the following three conditions have been met:

1. The message is received and understood precisely as meant by the sender;
2. The message has been approved by the receiver and followed-up by actions desired by the sender;
3. There are no obstacles to do whatever has to be done to follow-up on the message sent.

Characteristics of effective communication

According to Tubbs and Moss (1974), effective communication must fulfill five conditions: *understanding, enjoyment, influencing attitude, better relationships, and action.*

1. *Understanding.* Understanding can only be achieved when two persons have the same interpretation of the same action. In the west nodding the head is interpreted as agreement while in India shaking the head is interpreted as agreement. This type of miscommunication will lead to the primary breakdown in communication. In order to avoid misunderstanding in interpersonal communication, three conditions must be fulfilled: credibility, attractiveness, and trustworthiness. Credibility depends on the person, the topic discussed and situation. Credibility depends on the perception of the receiver. A university professor might be highly respected by students, but will be eaten by crocodiles in a river. Attractiveness of a person will also influence credibility in a strong way. An attractive salesperson will probably be selling more products than an unattractive salesperson. Credibility and trustworthiness depends on expertise of a person: a medical doctor is given more credibility than a salesperson who is trying to make a sale by overemphasizing the good traits of a certain product. Credibility also depends on charisma or people who seem to possess exceptional abilities to lead and influence others. Finally, understanding depends heavily on the language used: words and body language.

2. *Enjoyment.* Not all communication is aimed towards exchanging information and building understanding. A simple "Good morning, how are you?" is not meant to gain information. This kind of communication is simply aimed to make another person feel good. These kind of sentences are meant to arouse feelings of warmth, friendship, and enjoyment of casual conversations.

3. *Influencing attitude.* Most often communication is undertaken to influence another person. Politicians would like to create a positive image towards the electorate to be

elected to public office. A teacher wants to persuade the students to love science more. Advertisers want to stimulate consumers to buy a certain product or service. A man wants to convince his girlfriend that he is good enough to love and to be loved. These activities are all aimed to persuade someone else. Persuasion can be described as the process of influencing opinions, attitudes, and actions of people by using psychological manipulations so that others will behave as intended by a certain person or group of persons.

4. *Better relationships.* Communication is also meant to develop good social relationships. Humans are social beings who cannot live alone. We want to interact with others in a positive way. Social needs are needs which to develop and maintain satisfactory relationships with others. We want to join others and form a relationship, we want to control and be controlled, and we want to love and to be loved. If we fail to develop positive interpersonal relationships, we might become aggressive, delusional, mentally and physically ill, and try to flight from reality. Anonymity will make people aggressive, inclined to steal and destroy, and loose all social responsibilities. It was mentioned earlier that primary communication breakdown is caused by misunderstanding. Secondary communication breakdown, in turn, is caused by inability to form positive relationships or "misrelationships".

5. *Action.* Persuasion is aimed towards realizing desired actions. Communication to create understanding is already difficult, but it is far more difficult to change attitude. Even more difficult is to make people act in a certain way. Making people act in a certain way is the most important indicator of effective communication. If we can change people that mean that we have been able to create understanding, change the attitude, and form a good relationship. Action is the cumulative result of the entire communication process. This does not only require understanding of all the psychological mechanisms in the communication process, but also understanding of the factors influencing human behavior.

Improving effective communication in social settings

In social settings, people communicate according to their basic nature which is aggressive, passive, or assertive (Liaw, 2005). The basic nature of people will become very obvious during interaction with others; when they speak and act in relation to others. When observing the three types of behavior, certain patterns can be discovered. With these patterns in mind, it is possible to respond in an appropriate manner to facilitate better communication. Let us look at these three types of people.

How to communicate with *aggressive* people

People who are aggressive believe that everybody should be like them, they are innocent, and have all the rights in the world while others do not. These people are closed-minded, bad listeners, not open to other views, like to interrupt, and like to dominate conversations. They achieve their goals by sacrificing others, dominating, condescending, forcing, and being sarcastic. They like to belittle others, shift the blame to others, intrude in private spaces, being the boss, know it all, and not respecting others. Their body language consists of pointing their fingers, stiff posture, hard and critical voice, and speaking fast and in fragments. They want to win all the time, threatening, and attacking. Their feelings are full of anger, animosity, frustration, and impatience. In short, these people make other people irritated and their behavior will cause impatience and intolerance. The best way to communicate with aggressive people is to let them speak until they are satisfied. Keep serious eye contact. You will need more time to communicate with them because it is difficult to deliver to people who think they know it better than you do. Avoid giving too many responses; they will become more passionate if they feel that are getting positive support and feedback. Avoid disagreeing with them. However, avoid agreeing with something which is definitely wrong. If there is an opportunity to say something, praise them and add your opinion in a gentle way. Try to say it quickly to avoid being cut off. Your praises will make them feel good and give you an opportunity to mention your message. Avoid speaking too fast or slow because aggressive people are impatient types. Do not feel offended by these people because they cannot help themselves. Understand this before starting to communicate with them.

It is not easy to communicate with aggressive people. If we are impatient, new confrontations will emerge. If you gain a better understanding of aggressive people, it will become easier to understand their strengths and weaknesses. With the right mixture of skills and experience, it is easier to "conquer" an aggressive person without going into heated debates.

How to communicate with *passive* people

Passive people are completely the opposite of aggressive people. They do not like others to expose their true feelings, cause conflicts, and disagree. They communicate in an indirect way, always complying without talking a lot. They are forgiving, giving others more trust than themselves, closed-minded about their wants and feelings, and leaving decisions to others. They complain a lot, agree with everybody to avoid conflicts, show silent responses when treated unfairly, and have a hard time implementing something. Their body language consists of nodding and smiling all the time, eyes facing the floor, sloughing posture, soft and complaint voice, speaking fast when worried, but slowly when in doubt. They try to avoid confrontations at all cost, agree too often, and seek a lot of advices and supervision. They feel helpless, hopeless, dependent, viewless, and characterless causing them to be disliked by other people.

The best way to communicate with passive people is to deliver messages in a brief way and directly to the point because these people cannot digest a lot of information. Always ask their opinion because they are reluctant to say what they think.

Tell them that you appreciate their opinions. Stimulate them talk more by using open questions like "how" and "why." Avoid using a loud voice and speaking fast because they might be startled and reluctant to say more. Ask them to have eye contact during conversations to get better results.

It is not easy to communicate with passive people. Their ignorance and unhappy posture will cause boredom. For this reason it is important to stimulate and motivate them to talk more with different variations by praising them repetitively. This will raise their self-esteem and slowly they will improve their communication skills.

How to communicate with *assertive* people

As mentioned in previous chapters, assertiveness is the best communication style because it is an accommodative style. Assertive people are looking for things which people have in common. They value their own self-esteem and rights and that of others. They do not want to win all arguments, but want to handle all situations effectively. They listen carefully, determine boundaries and hopes, base opinions on facts and not on opinions, expose themselves directly and honestly, and monitor the feelings of others. They avoid being judgmental, subjective and suspicious because they have a high self-esteem, flexible character and accommodative style of communicating. They are funny, proactive, consistent, full of initiatives, and realistic about their goals. They try to achieve their goals without violating the rights of others. Their body language is open and natural with attentive facial expressions. They always have eye contact; a good voice in terms of volume and they can speak with different speed depending on the situation. When dealing with confrontations they negotiate, bargain, and compromise. They avoid negative feelings and always try to express enthusiasm, high self-esteem, high self-motivation, and know where they stand.

The best way to communicate with assertive people is to appreciate them by stating that your views might be theirs also. Deliver detailed and clear messages because they are good listeners. Avoid judging people because they value opinions of others. Give them time to expose their thoughts calmly and chronologically. Use different voice tones or intonations because they like that. Give several alternatives when you offer something because they do not like rigidity. Speak confidently so that you can match their confidence.

By using the above tips, it is possible to communicate with assertive people longer and more focused. They value commonality and competencies of others. Avoid topics which will invite appraisals of unfairness like the character of people not present or things which cannot be measured. They love peace, but are firm about things already agreed before. Do not play games about these things because they are very serious about them.

INTELLIGENT COMMUNICATION

In 1983, Gardner published his book on multiple intelligences. It swept through the world of education like a whirlwind and was widely announced as the new paradigm. New insights were added about learning styles caused by these so-called different intelligences. Soon after came more insights called 'emotional intelligence', 'social intelligence', and 'spiritual intelligence'. Before the waves of intelligences, the academic world was swept of its feet by 'rationality'. Before we can be intelligent, we had to be rational first, otherwise the world might slip into chaos. Before rationality, it was 'planning' which was the magic lamp of Aladdin. How could we do anything without planning? Despite all these wonderful scientific insights, the world still has enough weapons to kill itself several times. Conflicts and wars seem to be the order of the day, instead of planned, rational, and intelligent lifestyles. Perhaps we need to invent something called 'intelligent communication' first before we can create a better world for everyone. What is exactly intelligent communication? Here is a summary:

1. **Intrapersonal reflections: ask yourself why you are communicating; what are your objectives?** Your effectiveness in communication will be improved considerably if you listen carefully, think and formulate sentences in your head before

saying them, List your practical and objective goals in order of priority: What major problems do you want to solve? What caused you to be in this situation in the first place? You must constantly think about the objectives of others. Through knowing the traits of human nature and others' needs and goals, you will be able to step into their shoes and determine what to do next.

2. **Neutralize negative feelings and thoughts before engaging yourself in positive and constructive communication situations.** Before delivering messages with a strong negative tone or undertone, you must realize that these messages will have a great impact on your listeners. When you are angry, count to ten before speaking. When you are very angry, count to 100 before speaking. This will eliminate any outburst and give you the awareness that you will need to proceed.

3. **Talk clearly when you communicate; use your voice optimally**. About 38 percent of a listener's first impression of us will be based on how we sound. Our voice influences people's first impressions of us and the message they ultimately receive. When others speak with a flat, monotonous, condescending, pompous, and pretentious voice, we switch off. When the voices we hear are hearty, powerful or passionate, we sit up and take notice.

4. **Empathize or try to understand the point of view of the other person**. Most people do not realize it, but empathy is a skill and like any skill, we need to practice it. This means exploring the situation with the other person and asking questions; checking your empathy by using your own words what you perceive the other person's beliefs and position to be; and realistically imagining what it would be like to be in their position and feel the way they do. We need to practice empathy until it comes naturally and automatically to us.

5. **Look for your own body language: try to avoid negative signals**. The right body language helps us gathering and giving quality information. Of course it is our intention to send sensible verbal and nonverbal messages at all levels. The more we concentrate on our own body language, the more control we have over the nonverbal messages we are sending to others and thus over the communication process itself. The better we manage our body language, the stronger our communication will become.

6. **Look for the body language of the other person; try to pick up negative signals**. Most of us read others' body language instinctively and quickly, and the conclusions we reach often go straight into our subconscious. It is beneficial to look out for certain positive and negative signals. We can then adjust how we are sending our message. Our communication will inevitably be more successful. (see chapter 6)

7. **Interpersonal skills: try to be cooperative when communicating**. A lot of people want to win most of their communication encounters. They will then moralize, play psychologist, talk about the past, or speak with a sarcastic tone. The result will be frustration. We need to avoid this and seek for cooperation by building rapport through matching our own and their choice of words and communication style. Listen with empathy, use neutral words and tone of voice.

8. **Go for the best outcome: try to get the most out of your communication situation**. Always conclude by saying something positive about some part of the

encounter. Let your partner know how much you appreciated what you both have solved. Talk about what you look forward to. Being a gracious, graceful, accessible, available person really pays off.

9. **Engage in fruitful conversation: try to make your conversations meaningful.** Before offering your solutions, ask what the other person needs, wants, objects to, or has a problem with. By doing this you will become a non-threatening, positive communicator. This will give you the right direction for your pitch. Make use of the formula by speaking to the interests of others and then people will listen to you.

10. **Neutralize negative expressions of the other; try to eliminate miscommunication.** Even during important communication settings, a lot of people are unable to push any other thoughts from their minds. They will then be unable to focus wholly on the other person and what they are saying. Focusing on the speaker will improve communication significantly because it helps him/her to give good information. It will also help us improve our ability to hear it. Do not forget to orient your body towards the other person which will encourage the other person to continue.

11. **Talk in a symmetric fashion: try not to talk down or up.** A lot of people replace asking with telling, demanding, commanding, forcing, and railroading. This will lead to resistant responses. Telling is a pushy way of communicating which will cause rebellion. Asking, in turn, is based on mutual respect and facilitates discussion. Asking will open up avenues of collaborating or reaching a compromise to achieve a win-win outcome. Asking reflects the fact that the other person has choices and people will become happy communicators when there is a choice. They will think that their words are recognized. In the end, asking is a very easy habit to learn.

12. **Concentrate on your own words: try to use political correct language.** Most people will respond defensive and even hostile when hearing words full of negative emotions or phrases with negative undertones? Most people will resent these socalled impartial words and phrases when they are delivered in a hostile voice tone or as a command. For this reason using neutral tone of voice and language are important to put the listener at ease. Listeners need to feel that they are not being attacked. They will feel more confident when they hear objective, frank, factual, descriptive words, phrases and tones of voice. They will certainly be encouraged to listen. Communication should be constructive all the time by emphasizing fact gathering and problem solving.

13. **Overcome communication barriers.** As mentioned in chapter 3, the communication barriers are formidable. However, we all have our own unique set of obstacles. Communication will definitely become effective if we are aware of them and we genuinely want to overcome them. Overcoming communication barriers requires a lot of patience and understanding of the specific obstructions experienced by the other person. Successful communication can only be achieved when obstacles are recognize and dealt with adequately. Mutual understanding is the best medicine against obstacles and this can best be achieved through asking questions, revising your messages, and speaking more slowly or loudly.

14. **Meet your own expectations/objectives.** Do you want others to control your behavior? Do you let others pull the strings all the time? If yes, then you are suffering from a low self-esteem. You let others choose your behavior because they are in

control of you. Do not allow to happen. You can take charge of your communications to get the results you want. It is important to keep your locus of control internal if you want to choose the way you act and communicate. If you can control your own behavior, you can largely direct the result of any communication in which you engage. Try to develop a higher self-esteem so that you can decide what to say and do.

15. **Meet the expectations/objectives of the other**. There are two ways to communicate with each other: (1) tearing others down to build yourself up: (2) bringing out the best in others. The second method is based on learning, sharing ideas, and gaining valuable experience. The second method is usually used by people with high selfesteem who are always trying to improve others' confidence. They are generous with praise because they want to others to feel good about themselves. Praises will be processes by the human brain in such a way that neuropeptides and endorphins in both the giver and the receiver are released. Complimenting each other will make us all feel good!

16. **Unblock conversation stoppers: try to keep the conversation going**. Conversations are subjected to the iron law of psychological reciprocity. People will naturally respond in tune with the treatment they get. If you meet a friendly person who is constantly smiling, you will definitely give up being unhelpful or uncooperative. This will always happen. Just look around in restaurants, car parks, shops and offices and you will see it happening every single day. However, if you give someone else a bad treatment, do not be surprised if you get the same treatment back. Behavior breeds behavior.

17. **Negotiate wisely: try to find a win-win solution.** Most negotiators lose their attention on their primary goals which they can control or influence. This will cause confusion and inability to achieve goals and finding a win-win solution. Always keep your goals in mind when negotiating. If your goals are very ambitious (large) or longterm, divide them up into smaller steps which are feasible. Express your goals in specific measurable terms. Always keep your goals realistic and challenging.

18. **Introspect or ask yourself: am I communicating effectively?** A lot of people are reluctant to admit that they are talking to themselves all the time. But, according to psychologists, we talk to ourselves more than 50,000 times a day! Self-talk is a powerful way to change our self-esteem. A lot of people are overwhelmed by their feelings of nervousness. They will tell themselves not to get nervous. This is an ineffective method. By talking to yourself to stay calm, you will be able to really stay calm in difficult situations. When you want to remember to do something, do not program yourself to not forget, but to remember. Self-talk can be considered to be the silent messages we give ourselves throughout the day. It strongly influences our behavior because it directly reflects our self-esteem and self-image. A lot of people think that others determine their emotions while in reality we are in control of our own emotional state.

19. **Commit yourself to the promises you made**. Do not make promises you cannot keep! If you made promises, you need to realize them and keep your word. The bad habits of sitting back passively and waiting for things to happen must be stopped. The first thing you have to do is figuring out what you need to do in order to realize the

promises you made. If you made promises you need to become a proactive person. By demonstrating your proactive attitude, you show that you can design your own future. Do not assume that others or possible future events will realize your goals. It is important to stop procrastinating and to act in order to fulfill your promises and become known as a reliable person.

20. **Action must be taken after giving your commitment**. Once you have made a commitment, do not become pessimistic by the many difficulties, but try to find creative ways to overcome them. Al lot of people will make up excuses and fail to act. They blame the economy, the budget which is set too high, lack of money, other people, etc. What needs to be done is a rational assessment of the situation, identify the obstacles which may prevent you from achieving your goals, take the necessary steps to overcome them, and really remove those obstacles. It is important to keep on focusing your attention, energies, and efforts on things you can control and shape.

21. **Try to find common ground or consensus, not conflict**. Our own frame of reference is a combination of past experiences, our beliefs and values. The way we communicate is highly influenced by these three factors. We need to understand and if necessary change our frame of reference if we want to reach consensus with others. We also need to understand the frame of reference of others. We need to try to understand where they come from and what is important to them. This process of understanding someone else's frame of reference will take compassion. However, the effort is worth it because the more we understand others, the easier it is to communicate with them.

22. **Improve your communication skills on a continuous basis**. A lot of people usually try to pretend not to make mistakes or justify actions that have lead them to make mistakes. If we are not willing to change these bad habits, learning new communication skills will become nearly impossible. The more we try new things, the more likely we are to make mistakes because we are doing things we have never done before. We improve skills by trying new things, communicating in new ways, and continuously learning. Commit yourself to learn what each mistake has taught you about improving your communication skills. Making mistakes is a good reason to try again until you succeed. In other words, 'practice makes perfect'.

23. **Organize many encounters with others: try to get as much communication experience as you can.** People focus on different things; they are convinced in different ways and have unique working styles. If we observe and listen carefully, we can connect with others because we try to understand their basic psychological programming. People can be avoiders or seekers, knowledgeable or ignorant, matchers or mismatchers. People's brains operate in different ways resulting in dissimilar ways of making decisions, setting goals, taking action, finding proof, categorizing and sorting information. Once you have discovered how others think and act it going to be very useful to select your most effective communication strategy. Otherwise you will be speaking at cross-purposes due to a bad choice of strategy.

24. **Never stop learning from your positive and negative communication experiences**. After making a silly mistake, the first thing you want to do is hide from your embarrassing mistake. Learn from your mistakes! A lot of people do not forgive themselves after making a mistake. For this reason, self-forgiveness is an important

part of learning because it allows us to calm down and pay more attention to exactly what we are doing and precisely how we are doing it. Adopting a habit of empathetic forgiveness toward yourself will teach you about improving from the so many small mistakes. Each day will offer new opportunities to become a more successful communicator. If we learn from the small mistakes and become more observant and attentive, we will be able to avoid making those same mistakes in the future.

It is obvious that the above 24 tips can be summarized as: I.N.T.E.L.L.I.G.E.N.T. C.O.M.M.U.N.I.C.A.T.I.O.N.

How to communicate with left-brain and right-brain people

In the last few centuries, the function of the brain has been studies intensively from many different perspectives. One of the most recent discoveries is the existence of the left and right hemispheres of the brain which have specific functions. It has been discovered that the way certain people act is somehow connected to a certain hemisphere of their brains. For this reason certain people are either quiet, meditative, and contemplative while others are talkative or highly extrovert (Liaw, 2005).

How to communicate with *left-brain* people

People who are using the left hemisphere of their brain are more inclined to use logic and facts. They like to think more rationally than use their emotions in their daily lives. They do not like to even stop considering things which cannot be explained in a logical way; they inherently dislike irrational things. For this reason they are very interested in exact sciences like mathematics, chemistry, physics, and engineering. Furthermore they are very good in languages. They critically choose their words when communicating; using only those words which accurately represents their ideas without using any other words. In other words, they do not like to use many flowery words which in their opinion are not necessary. They like to explain something with great detail and accurate chronology focusing on the past and the present. What happened in the past and what is happening now are the central themes in their topics of discussion. The past is an important guide for the future. They have a strong memory especially if they have to recall names of concrete objects which played a big role in their lives. Their explanations will include many details like exact dates and places of events in the past and present.

Left-brain persons are inclined to show a stiff appearance because they consider logic more important than the social aspects of society in general. They consider systems and methodologies more important than outcomes from processes. They are smart persons who do not have the ability to cheer things up because they are introverts. In short, they are serious and analytical in nature and certain strategic moves are needed to communicate with them: avoid too much talking, use a systematic style of explaining with an opening, middle part, and an ending, provide sufficient facts and data, use relevant words which they can use to analyze our expertise in a certain area, avoid to much body language, use scientific approaches, control cheerfulness, give them time to evaluate your messages, and give them time to respond before continuing with the next sentence. It is important to realize that leftbrain people are difficult to communicate with because they seem cold and uninterested which are caused by their neurological system. By using the techniques mentioned above, it is possible to communicate effectively with left-brain persons. Avoid gossiping with them because they consider accountable facts and data to be very important.

How to communicate with *right-brain* people

Right-brain people are completely the opposite of left-brain people. They are warm and kind persons who seem temperamental at times. When communication with them, make sure that you give similar cheerful responses, talk about many social and humanistic topics, avoid facts and data as much as possible, use words to express feelings, use a lot of metaphors because they are superb visualisers, praise them a lot, avoid talking about the past which are only memories to them, and limit talking about small stuff and details.

If starting a conversation with left-brain people, begin with social anecdotes or the merits of their families or their artistic interior decorations. They like to begin with any social topic and then it will become easier to talk about the issues you want to discuss with them.

TEN COMMANDMENTS OF EFFECTIVE COMMUNICATION

Everything we do is communication. Without communication we will not be able to interact in a civilized manner. Without communication we will not be able to create modern societies. Without communication we would not be able to create prosperity for ourselves. Without communication we would not be able to construct organizations necessary for the reproduction of material wealth. Communication is the most important building block of human civilization.

In his "theory of communicative action" (1984; 1987), Habermas introduces two separate spheres in the social reality: 'system' and 'lifeworld'. He argues that in modern western societies, politics and economics have differentiated themselves from the lifeworld, which consists of the 'private sphere' (households and private organizations) and the 'public sphere' (parliament, parties, the press, etc.). According to Habermas, system is the domain of material reproduction which requires a certain kind of rationality: the 'cognitiveinstrumental.' The lifeworld, on the other hand, is the domain of symbolic reproduction, which is realized through the use of 'communicative' rationality. This 'first-order' differentiation, or structural differentiation, is not necessarily problematic, since an economic subsystem is essential for the growth welfare and a political subsystem is necessary for efficient public administration.

From the perspective of the lifeworld, the relations with the economic system are realized through four roles. Citizens in the private sphere exchange relations as employees and consumers, whereas citizens in the public sphere form relations with the administrative system as citizens and clients. The system cannot secure its existence without extracting the 'raw materials' from the lifeworld in the form of labor, economic demand, taxes and mass loyalty. The lifeworld, in turn, depends on the system through incomes from employment, goods, and services, organizational accomplishments and political decisions. The 'raw materials' of the lifeworld can, however, only be made suitable for the system by 'mediatization': the rather violent reproduction of production factors suitable for exchanges with system products. Mediatization by the economic system is achieved by 'monetarization' and mediatization by the administrative system is achieved by 'bureaucratization'. The modernization of the lifeworld remains a positive process as long as efficiency and material reproduction are regenerated for the benefit of society as a whole. It will, however, become problematic when money and power mediums enter the lifeworld to replace communicative action (necessary for symbolic reproduction) with purposive-rational action (necessary for material reproduction). This is what Habermas means by 'colonization'. The consequences of colonization are loss of cultural traditions, solidarity and socialization.

Although the colonization of the lifeworld is happening is modern societies, Habermas does not believe that this is an inevitable fact of life. He believes that a lot of people may be captured by economic and political ways of thinking, but still have one strong weapon to resist: language. Language makes it possible for people to communicate with each other to reach agreements about facts, standards and values. Habermas is optimistic about the ability of people to reach rational agreements with the use of language. Evidence of the use of language to initiate social changes can be found in the activities of social movements. Habermas did not formulate a strategy to cope with the problem of colonization, but as a scientist, he was convinced that this problem can be resolved by a new paradigm which is actually his own theory: "the theory of communicative action."

If communication is so important then this implies a certain competency level in the strategies and tactics of communication possessed by all people irrespective of their education, social background, nationality, and common language. This is unfortunately not true because a large number of people do not have the proper communication skills necessary to become successful. Most of them are simply muddling through their daily lives using basic communication skills which are barely enough to keep their heads above the water. What are actually the characteristics of good communicators?

CHARACTERISTICS OF GOOD COMMUNICATORS

Good communicators pay attention to everything the other person is communicating

Poor communicators focus on their own self interests: thoughts, feelings, experiences and ideas. They are not really interested in quality communication with others. Good communicators, on the other hand, looks carefully to everything the other person is communicating: symbolic, nonverbal and verbal. We are constantly trying to communicate our self-image and self-esteem. We do this by driving an expensive sport car, live in a personally designed house, wearing designer clothes and wear expensive jewellery. Or we might do just the opposite! These attributes are merely reflecting how we feel about ourselves and how we wish to be treated by others. These communications may be sent and received unconsciously. Good communicators are trained to pay attention to these things and translate that into the thoughts, feelings, and aspirations of others. Good communicators know what others are trying to communicate and what hold importance and worth to others. They look at the personal items put on the desk of others at work, how they change their posture, seating position or facial expression; all small things which express something about others' attitudes and feelings.

Good communicators constantly think about the nature of their messages.

A lot of poor communicators speak in undiplomatic ways: they barge right in by using their mouths before using their brain. Good communicators, on the other hand, will think carefully first about how, when and where they will deliver a message, especially important messages. One of the most effective techniques to communicate effectively is to frame a message in a clever manner: with an analogy, a fact, an anecdote? They apply the formula by imagining how they can make the other person understand the point they want to make. This is done by thinking about something which is important to the other person so that they can relate to him/her. They think about their main goals and what they want to achieve from a particular communication setting. They think before they say something.

Good communicators always try to find the right combination of words, body language, dress, and tone of voice before sending a message.

Poor communicators do not think about how to deliver a message. They just say what they need to say and leave understanding and interpretation to the poor listener. Poor communicators are not interested in finding the optimal mix of words, body language and tone of voice. Good communicators, on the other hand, think first before they communicate. They do this with more concentration when the communication is an important one. Good communicators know that people use a variety of senses to listen and interpret our messages. Therefore good communicators match their body language with the signals they want to send. Good communicators dress appropriately and watch their tone of voice. These things are always important factors if a message wants to be received in the proper way. Good communicators realize that how we say something is often more important than what we say.

Good communicators try to avoid using the same words when sending their message to different persons because no one person is identical.

Poor communicators are not very flexible because they will say the same thing to ten different people the same way each time. They do not realize that those ten people have different levels of understanding, backgrounds and desires. Then they are often truly amazed by the fact that no one 'got it.' Poor communicators do not realize that messages can be received in different ways opposite to what they expected. This is caused by the difference between the intention we put in our messages and the way others read the intentions behind our messages. Good communicators are always investigating what the other person perceives to be important. Good communicators try to link the information they already have about the other to their messages. Good communicators use their communication experience with the other as an effective guide to design new messages. With these techniques, good communicators can frame their message so it suits with the other person's thoughts, feelings and aspirations. They also monitor the other person's reactions while they are delivering their messages. If necessary, they adjust the style of delivery to facilitate effective communication.

Good communicators are always ready to be flexible or try to move on after delivering their message by reaching a decision, solving a problem, negotiating a compromise, etc.

Poor communicators think the communication is over when they have said their bit. Poor communicators always think that they must state their own point of view clearly, fairly and persuasively without realizing that this is ineffective communication; it is a one-way street. Good communicators know that before effective communication occurs, they need to know the interests of the other by carefully listening to other person's point of view. This helps them state their point of view effectively. After gathering and giving good information, good communicators are ready to move on; reaching a decision, solving a problem, negotiating a compromise, winning a sale, making a friend, resolving a disagreement, reaching an agreement, concluding a deal, etc.

Good communicators are fully aware of the reciprocal nature of communication which is a process of giving and receiving a message.

Poor communicators have never learned the basic process of giving and taking as part of effective communication. Poor communicators do not possess the skills to suit the other person or the circumstances. Effective communication is actually much more than just giving and receiving a message. Effective communication happens between and among people. It is a reciprocal process in which sender and receiver do it together like a dance. Like in any classical dance it means leading and following. Good communicators are basically superb dancers!

Although the above typical characteristics seem to be obvious and easy to understand, many people have difficulties applying them in a consistent manner. Communication is a process which is comparable to driving a car. The more you do it, the better driver you will become. Experience is the best teacher in communication. Moreover, the willingness to learn from your experiences is very important. Of course we make mistakes, but we try to learn from those mistakes and become better next time.

Having explained the above characteristics of good communicators, what are the ten commandments of effective communication?

TEN COMMANDMENTS OF EFFECTIVE COMMUNICATION

1. **Always try to give feedback based on facts and not on opinions and/or emotions which might upset or offend the other person.** When we give either positive or negative evaluations, we are treading slippery waters. This is especially so when we comment on others in a general rather than specific way. Before you know it, others might receive a compliment as patronizing flattery. In turn, when giving constructive comments, the other might interpret them as belittling criticism. We might unconsciously think that we are in some way better than others when we pass a positive or negative judgment. Offer sincere praise in a respectful way to avoid sounding superior. Try to use the words of the other when giving a constructive critique. Always try to be sincere and let the others know that you are truly sincere.

2. **Always try to empathize or to see a situation from the other's point view.** A lot of people are easily tempted to point out the faults of others and when that happens the situation worsens because the past is mentioned again by recalling all their past deeds we disapprove of. This is not way to communicate effectively and constructively. We need to explore the situation of others through reflective listening. We need to control our urge to give advice and wait for them to ask for advice if they want it. Poor communicators rapidly close cordial communication encounters by preaching, blaming, shaming, and dragging up the past. Good communicators try to accept the other person's views without preaching and/or moralizing. Why do a lot of people preach? This is because they think they know it better, have more adequate

experience, and superior values. A lot of people get carried away with these believes and easily become serious and high-minded with someone. Since we can never know another person's frame of reference fully, it is likely that from their point of view at least, our preaching will not be welcome. Instead of preaching, it is better to walk a mile in their shoes. The more this is done, the less likely people will moralize. Instead, appreciating, empathizing and accepting will become the productive habits. Blaming and shaming are two other common types of moralizing. It happens a lot that if someone makes a mistake, he/she is scolded and this will certainly make him/her feel awful. Instead, it is far more productive to show them what he/she did wrong and how to do it right next time. It should be realized that people neither make mistakes nor do things wrong on purpose. For this reason, is a much better option to focus on the future and helping others to decide what to do next time.

3. **Criticize using neutral language and tone of voice**. It is dangerous to diagnose people or their behavior by using a certain language or tone of voice. First of all, we have no way of knowing whether we're right or wrong, Chances are big that our diagnosis is wrong! Once we made a diagnosis the situation becomes worse because tend to use a judging tone of voice and patronizing language. This will definitely lead to all kinds of difficulties in communication. Some things are best left unsaid. If you must say something, say it clearly and respectfully by using neutral language and tone of voice. Using the 'I' language will be the most appropriate way.

4. **Say what you mean without becoming sarcastic**. Sarcasm will definitely rub us the wrong way at times. According to Gerard Nierenberg, sarcasm can be identified as the 'meta-message' which describe the message-behind-the-message. Meta messages reveal the underlying and real meaning behind the words. Sarcasm is in the same league as name-calling, ridiculing and shaming. It will inhibit open communication, worse even; it will usually lead to negative results. Hurting others' feelings is easily established with sarcasm. Instead of resorting to sarcasm, it is much more fruitful to state your point clearly and considerately. It is much more effective to ask questions rather than dismiss someone's ideas.

5. **If you want something from others, ask, don't command**. Commanding is when we are telling others what to do in a way that leaves them no room for discussion. Commanding closes avenues to seek further information, disagree or even agree. When hearing a command the other person will feel more like a machine than a person. Commands will result in either an aggressive response or a resentful submission. This will depend on our relative status and their state of mind. Instead use empathy and express the messages in such a way that the other person will find it easy to understand why something should be done in a specific way. Better even, give suggestions for enhancement. If possible, focus on the end result and let others decide which means are the best.

6. **Give the other person a chance to speak, do not slip into 'railroading.'**Railroading can be defined as subtle form of commanding. We politely make statements which sound logical and we assume the other person agrees. We do not give them a genuine opportunity to express their point of views. The situation becomes worse when we try to make the other yield our point of view by keeping the conversation moving along very rapidly. Instead we should look for verbal and

nonverbal gestures pointing at the other person's acceptance. Slow down and give the other person a chance to speak. Don not hesitate to pause and ask whether they agree with you, or if they have any thoughts they can add.

7. **Explain why something needs to happen, don't threaten**. Most people will always look for ways to defend themselves against threats. Threats can be direct or subtle with the 'or else' implied in their message. Threats will usually widen the communication gap and a person threatened will look for ways to ignore the threat and disobey. It is much more productive to explain why something needs to happen with sounding threatening. Replace threats with the 'I' language and simply explain why someone should or should not do something. If necessary, explain the consequences, accurately and fairly. Encourage rather than threaten.

8. **Don't give advice or opinions if people don't ask for it.** Try to avoid giving advice or opinions when others are not asking for it. By popping out phrases like "You should/you ought to/have you tried" you are basically forcing your advice or opinions upon others. Consequently, others will ignore you, making what you say hot air.

9. **Be to the point, avoid vagueness at all cost**. People are not mental telepaths. If you do not go straight to the point, others have to guess what you really want to say or want. This is an impossible situation and you force others to guess wrong most of the time. "I" messages are good and effective techniques to avoid confusion..

10. **Don't talk down or up to others; avoid diverting the conversation to trivial matters.** When a conversation becomes emotional or personal, or when another person begins to reveal something of their true self, some people feel uncomfortable and try to bring the conversation back to insignificant matters. This leads to such behaviors as distracting the speaker, changing the subject or responding in formulas. Instead, listen to what is being said. The person is confiding in you. The least you can do is hear them out.

How to communicate with people with different communication styles

All normal humans are born with the five senses: seeing, hearing, tasting, smelling, and touching. All these five senses have different functions which help us function optimally in our daily lives. Not all human beings use those five senses with the same intensity; some use their eyes more often than their ears whereas others use their noses more often than their eyes. This can be seen very clearly with many people; those who love music will use their ears more often than others. Someone who likes paintings, in turn, will use his or her eyes more often than their other sensory organs. In communication, people absorb information with different sensory perceptions: eyes, ears, tongues, noses or skins. Realizing these different sensory perceptions and using them as a guide will help communication become more effective. There are basically four types of communication styles: visual, auditory, kinesthetic, and digital (Liaw, 2005).

Communicating with *visual* persons

These persons are more inclined to use visual words in their conversations like seeing, emerging, pointing, exposing, dreaming, etc. These words all represent visual images which pop up in their brains. If you communicate with these persons, you will instantly recognize them because they will use their imagination to make pictures in their descriptions. For this reason they will always explain something by describing the physical shapes of things. If they are explaining a car, they will say that it is a vehicle with four wheels and an engine in front as the source of energy. A person who uses his or her ears to communicate will not be able to do this. Visual persons use their eyes in interpersonal communication; they can imagine things and describe them with a lot of accuracy. They like to see concrete than abstract things which they can realistically imagine in their brains. When communication with visual people emphasize visual words, avoid auditory words, use pictures when explaining something, use a lot of relevant body language, use more expressive gestures, and avoid long silences.

Communicating with *auditory* persons

Auditory persons are more inclined to use their ears than their eyes. They prefer to use auditory words when communicating: 'it sound good" or "the music really sounds good."

When communicating with auditory persons it is important to use a lot of auditory words, avoid visual words, use a clear voice, use the correct rhythm of speech (not too fast or slow), and use a lot of articulate words. These persons really enjoy communication with their ears and it is important to control your voice when communicating with them. Voices which are gentle and medium sound will capture their attention which will be interpreted as sympathetic persons by them. They sometimes close their eyes to enjoy the sound of the voice of the person speaking to them. Whispering in their ears will most certainly be an effective way to communicate with them.

Communicating with *kinesthetic* persons

Kinesthetic persons are more inclined to use their body movements, feelings and other aspects related to emotions. These people will more often use words like "I feel", "I am touched", and 'I can feel." They also close their eyes at times to really understand the words spoken to them. They are very emotional and sensitive; they really focus on the movements of others. When communication with kinesthetic persons uses emotional words (feeling, sad, disappointment, anger, etc), combine words with the relevant body language, touch them if necessary, and give emotional support with comforting words. They really like hear emotional words and sentences like "I can understand you" which will make a more lasting effect on them. They will closer to you when you touch them either during difficult times or when they have performed well. These techniques will make them your best friend for a long time.

Communicating with *digital* persons

Digital persons are more inclined to focus their attention on words. Their language is often without senses because their words convey thought and reflection. Digital persons look down and to their left a lot when thinking; speak in well modulated, slow-paced, low tones, ad gesture minimally. A digital person hum or sing a lot, enjoy conversations with people, rather talk than write a paper, pay attention at lectures and speeches, and pay more attention to what people say than how they look. When communicating with digital persons present your information orally (voicemail, discussions, phone conversations), tell the truth, have good and long conversations with them, choose your words carefully, and avoid pictures, sounds or feelings. Digital people are objective, specific, logical, and accurate. They are actually quite 'dry' people.

PUBLIC SPEAKING? BE PREPARED!

Speeches and presentations require a few special communication techniques because they are delivered orally, usually in public circumstances. Preparing speeches or oral presentations is actually similar to delivering any other interpersonal message. You need to define your purpose, analyze the audience, and develop a plan for presenting your points. Before these crucial steps of preparing a speech will be discussed, it is important to know the difference between the 4 main types of speeches.

FOUR MAIN TYPES OF SPEECHES

Traits of the memorized speech

The memorized speech is best suited for short talks. It is impossible to recall every word. Instead you need to memorize the ideas and concepts you want to get across. However, it is important to memorize the introduction carefully in order to sound relaxed and confident. This can actually be done for other types of speeches and not only for the memorized speech. Just remember, if you try to memorize a long talk, you may forget and panic.

Traits of the manuscript speech

The manuscript speech is usually delivered in longer more technical business presentations, meetings and conferences. The manuscript speech must be well researched and structured. Examples include a legal presentation, a parliamentary address, a press release or a speech. It is usually read so that it can be reported or quoted.

If you have to deliver manuscript speeches try to maintain eye contact by looking at your audience as often as possible while you are reading the manuscript. Reading and keeping eye contact with your audience the speech will be easier if you use wide margins, large type and double spacing. Avoid reading the entire speech without any eye contact because you will be speaking *at* the audience instead of speaking *to* the audience. This means that you also need to involve your audience through your body language: your facial expressions, eyes, and gestures. You want your audience to be interested in what you are saying. You do not want them to continually look at the top of your head as you are reading.

Traits of the prepared speech

Almost all speeches can be called prepared speeches because they are planned and organized before the time of presentation. It is most advisable to prepare an outline with notes that will act as prompts in the planning stage. The delivery of the speech will appear spontaneous and relaxed when you use the prompts well. It demonstrates that you have prepared properly and know how to express your ideas in an effective manner.

During the preparation, it is very helpful to note important ideas, phrases, quotations and statistics. It is really not necessary to write down every word. Try using different words you can think of on the spot at the time of presentation; this will increase spontaneity.

Avoid talking form a complete set of notes because this might cause you reading your speech word for word. This will definitely bore your audience! Make your speech interesting at all times by maintaining eye contact and reading the prepared speech as limited as possible. By maintaining eye contact, you can hold the audiences' interest and you will also be able to note the audience's response. This will help you to evaluate the effectiveness of the presentation. If you are making a prepared speech for the first time, two of the following useful aids must be used:

- overhead transparencies or power point slides, and

- palm or cue cards

You need to mention the main points in the overhead transparencies or power point slides. The main points outline the structure in your talk and acts as a prompt to keep your delivery to the organized points. The two advantages in using overhead transparencies are that they increase audience understanding and provide the speaker hidden notes. Another aid is prepared palm cards which should list the main points and include supporting information. Cue cards and notes help you to stay with the topic. Hold these in the palm of your left hand when you deliver the speech. They keep the outline of your speech clear. By looking at the main points in the cards or notes, you will ensure yourself that your statements are accurate.

Traits of the impromptu speech

As suggested by its name: the impromptu speech is a speech delivered unexpectedly and cannot be delivered with preparation. Impromptu speeches are typically delivered during special occasions or are delivered as courtesy speeches: welcomes, introductions, and acknowledgments. The element of surprise will always play a role when delivering these speeches despite having a lot of experience in public speaking. For this reason, it is important to think clearly, analyze the situation quickly, and speak briefly and to the point. When you start your speech, the following order of presentation is recommended:

- frankly state why you are giving the speech;

- indicate why your speech is relevant to the organization or audience;

- conclude with some of the characteristics of the individual or organization receiving the recognition.

HOW TO PREPARE YOUR SPEECH

How to define your purpose

Speeches are especially important in the world of work and business. You must master the skill of public speaking in your career because you will definitely be called on to give speeches and oral presentations for many different reasons. If you are working in the human resources department, you will definitely give the following speeches: orientation briefings to new employees and explanation of company policies, procedures, and benefits. If you are promoted to become a supervisor in a certain department, you must be ready to deliver training programs. If you decide to set up your own management consultancy, you must be ready to give analytical presentations on the advantages of different proposals. When asked to deliver a speech or presentation, it is important to determine the purpose of each speech. This will help you determine the relevant and appropriate style and content.

In the first stage which is the planning stage, establish the setting or context of the speech must be identified. This will help you a relevant speech which fulfills the specific task as well as the needs of the audience. Speeches will become relevant when they are designed to achieve one of three objectives below, or a combination of these three objectives:

1. To inform: when delivering an informative speech, you are expected to supplying facts or information based on facts illustrated with clear examples and supporting materials. The aim of this speech is to develop ideas, deliver information, and show how something works or can be done. When delivering this type of speech, it is important to find a balance between the content and the discussion. This is necessary to deliver a truly informative speech which is unbiased and objective;

2. To persuade: when delivering a persuasive speech, you are expected to identify a need of the audience and persuade this audience about the actions you argue are necessary to satisfy their particular need. When delivering this type of speech, your main goal is to influence the audience, to change their attitude or get their support for a specific point of view;

3. To entertain: when delivering an entertaining speech, you are expected to apply several different techniques such as humor, anecdotes, examples and quotations around a common theme. These techniques are crucial if you want the audience to enjoy your presentation. Effective public speaking can best be realized through a combination of informative or persuasive elements with entertainment.

In general, interaction between you and the audience will begin when you mention facts and figures that will increase the audience's understanding of the subject. Otherwise you can also offer arguments to support various conclusions or recommendations. Interaction between you as a speaker and the audience usually happens when there is a purpose. This purpose is commonly based on persuading the audience to take a particular action, solving a problem in a cooperative manner, or making a decision. Other methods to start the interaction process with your audience are by inviting the audience to express their needs, suggest solutions, and/or formulate conclusions and recommendations. Because persuasive and collaborate presentations involve so much audience interaction, you have relatively little control of the material. When you get new input or unexpected reaction, do not panic and try to answer or respond calmly. You must do this without your prewritten script. It is quite normal that during speeches or presentations, you need to accomplish several of these purposes simultaneously.

Once you have memorized the material, you must gain self-confidence by practicing. This is especially necessary if you do not have much experience with public speaking. When practicing in front of a mirror it can still be considered as dry swimming. You need to visualize the room filled with listeners. It is also useful to record your talk on tape and play it again to get optimal sound of voice, timing, phrasing, and emphasis. It would be better to videotape your talk and see yourself perform as your audience will. You will then also see how well you coordinate the visual aids with your talk.

How to analyze your audience

After determining the purpose of your speech, the next step consists of thinking about another basic element of your speech or presentation: the audience. The first thing you have to do is finding out what the size and background of your audience is. If the audience only consists of a small number of persons, it is going to be easy to involve audience members in your presentation. However, if your audience consists of more than 12 people, you need to realize that managing the interaction between you and the audience will become much more difficult. For this reason, it is better to choose a speech style where a lot of telling instead of asking will be the main method of delivery. The second aspect which needs consideration is your audience's likely reaction to your speech or presentation. Will they respond in a hostile, receptive, or indifferent manner to your words? This question can only be answered when you are honest about your relationship with the audience. Do they know you and respect your opinions? The answers to these questions will help you decide on the best way to organize and present your material.

How to plan your speech

When you have to plan an oral message or a written message, you are actually following the steps: Defining the main idea, constructing an outline, estimating the appropriate length, and deciding on the most effective style.

How to develop a main idea

Do not start with the details, but start with the big picture. Identify the main idea or theme that you want the audience to grasp. You can imitate advertisers who cunningly attract the attention of their customers by launching a one sentence slogan emphasizing the benefit of the product promoted. You can do the same thing by mentioning a one-sentence generalization that links your subject and purpose to the audience's frame of reference.

How to develop an Outline

After you have carefully crafted the main idea of your speech, you can start outlining your speech or presentation. The structure of your speech should all be connected to the subject, purpose, audience, and time allotted for your presentation. If you have to deliver a short speech of around ten minutes or less, you need to organize your thoughts in a similar way as drafting a letter or brief memo. If your speech involves routine information nr the latest news, simply use a direct approach. However, if your speech involves bad news or persuasion, the indirect approach will be the best method of delivery.

It is always the best way to start your speech with an introduction that arouses the audience's interest. Then give a preview of what's to come. In the body of your presentation, explain the 5 W1H (who, what, when, where, why and how) of your topic. At the end of your speech which will cover the last two paragraphs, repeat the main points of your message. Close with a strong statement which will be remembered by your audience.

Longer speeches and presentations are structured like reports. Use a direct style consistent with the topic if the purpose is to entertain, motivate, or inform. However, when the purpose of your speech is to analyze, persuade, or collaborate, a different style will be necessary.

Your material needs to be structured around conclusions, recommendations or a logical argument. Use a direct style if the audience is receptive and an indirect one if you expect resistance. You need to explain how you have structured your material at the beginning. Whether the speech is a short or long one, limit the number of main points to three or four. If you want to keep the audience's attention, only include the most useful, interesting, and relevant supporting evidence. You can also keep the audience interested by summarizing the point you have just made at the end of each section. Then explain how it fits into your overall framework; this will surely keep the audience awake.

How to estimate length

Usually you will be given a specific amount of minutes to deliver your speech or presentation. So it is important to tailor your material to the available time. Your outline can be used as good guide in estimating the length of your speech and the time you need to deliver it. Without speaking too fast or too slowly, you will probably speak at the rate of about 125 to 150 words a minute (or around 7,500 to 9,000 words per hour). This will be equal to 20 up to 25 double-spaced typed pages of text. If the average paragraph consists of around 125 to 150 words in length, you must be able to speak at a rate of approximately one paragraph per minute. Do not try to deliver a complex speech in a time frame which is too short. Don't squeeze a complex presentation into a period that is too brief. In contrast, do not draw out a simple talk any longer than necessary because this method might add length to your speech, but it will not add depth.

How to decide on the style

In general, you can use a casual approach when you are giving a speech to a small group in a small conference room. A casual approach will encourage audience participation; they would be able to interject comments during your speech. In this particular setting it is really important that you use a conversational tone; use notes to help you recall important details if necessary.

On the other hand, addressing a large audience will require a completely different style. Especially if the event is an important one, it is really necessary to adopt a more formal style. Examples of situations in which a formal style is the best method of delivery are: announcements about mergers, acquisitions, new products, financial results, and other business milestones.

How to develop formal speeches and presentations

If you have experience writing a formal report, you can use this experience to prepare a major speech or presentation because both are similar in terms of preparation and structuring. However, there is one important difference: the techniques used for writing reports must be adjusted to an oral communication channel. This will definitely become an opportunity and a challenge at the same time.

Why is it an opportunity? Because you will be given a unique chance to interact with the audience. If you speak in front of an audience, you can receive as well as transmit information. This situation will give you the opportunity to adjust the content and the delivery of your message as you go along. Consequently, you must audit your speech or presentation to make it clearer and more compelling. You can also benefit from the nonverbal signals sent by your audience to adjust your style and words.

It is also a great moment to ask your audience express their ideas so that both of you reach a mutually acceptable conclusion. However, flexibility from your part is extremely important if you want to get the benefits of oral speeches because you will definitely experience less control when the level of interaction with the audience is increased. You must be ready to hear an unexpected comment from a member of the audience forcing you to shift to a new line of thought. This will require great skill! You also have to realize that you need to continuously accommodate the limitations of your audience especially to avoid boredom.To prevent your audience from becoming bored or losing interest, make optimal use of the following special techniques when developing the various elements of your speech: the introduction, the body, the close, the question-and-answer period, and the visual aids.

MASTERING THE ART OF DELIVERY

The introduction

How to arouse interest of your audience

If you are an experienced public speaker, you know that connecting to the personal concerns of your audience is a crucial aspect of delivering effective speeches. You will instantly know which tried-and-true techniques will be the most appropriate in certain situations. The first thing an experienced public speaker will know is that the introduction must match with the overall tone of the entire speech. Begin with a light introduction when the occasion is supposed to be fun. However, avoid cute introductions when presenting real business in front of a group of executives. When you are discussing a serious problem, leave your jokes and personal anecdotes at home. Also avoid being overly dramatic when your speech is basically a routine oral report. Above all, stay natural because the average audience will become offended by a corny and staged commencement.

How to build credibility

It was mentioned above that arousing interest of your audience is an important aspect of public speaking. Building credibility is actually more important because your credibility will be damaged if you might make the mistake of making an overblown opening. Of course you want your audience to respect your opinion and like you as a knowledgeable person. Research shows that there is a strong correlation between persuasion and credibility: a speaker with high credibility is more persuasive than a speaker with low credibility. For this reason it is imperative to make your audience believe your credentials within the first few minutes. If you have successfully established your credentials, your audience will certainly be willing to listen to you. Of course; people will decide within a few minutes whether you're worth listening to.

In building credibility, you will experience fewer difficulties with a familiar and openminded audience. This type of audience will be willing to believe your credibility as long as you do not stick your foot in your mouth. Establishing credibility is relatively easy if you're speaking to a familiar, open minded audience. As long as you avoid sticking your foot in your mouth, you can safely use your reputation. It is going to be a much more difficult task to earn credibility from strangers. You need all your public speaking skills and experience to earn the confidence of a skeptical or antagonistic audience.

Previewing the speech

In the introduction of your speech, the following points must be mentioned: a one sentence summary of your main idea, the most important supporting points, and the order of presenting those main points. Basically inform your audience that "This is the topic and these are the points I will cover." Only after mentioning this framework, you can move on to the body of your speech. But know you can be sure about the level of understanding of your audience; they will be able to grasp the facts and figures related to your main idea.

The body of the speech

In the body of your speech, you want to thoroughly discuss the three to four main point mentioned in your introduction. Like mentioned earlier, just use the same structure in a letter, memo, or report, but you keep the words simple. Two goals must be fulfilled during presenting the body of your speech: (1) keeping the structure of your speech clear and concise; (2) the structure of your speech is adequate enough to keep your audience's attention.

Emphasizing the structure of the speech

You will notice that when you are presenting your main ideas, your audience will experience difficulties in seeing the relationship between them and this will have an impact on their ability to absorb your main ideas. This problem can be overcome by using transitions which will become very important in longer speeches. Do not forget to make your transitions clear so that your audience will pick them up. Repeating your key ideas in the transitions will also be an extremely effective technique to keep the audience's attention. Last but not least, use your body language! Make your transitions apparent by your gestures, changing your voice, or introducing a visual aid.

One of the big issues of public speaking is stage fright. This feeling of nervousness may be experienced before, during, or even at the end of a speech. Nervousness is a normal thing and even the best actors still experience it. Like mentioned earlier, practice makes perfect. So you need to rehearse over and over again until you feel that you are familiar with your material.

Public speaking experts have suggested the following other tips:

- Your confidence will increase if you have a real genuine interest in the topic. Even if your knowledge is insufficient about the topic, you can compensate that with preparing more material than necessary.

- Like mentioned earlier, you need to cultivate a positive self-image by seeing yourself as polished and professional. If you have a positive self-image, you will also have a positive image of your message. The audience will pick this up and really perceive you as a professional expert.

- Adopt a realistic attitude about stage fright. Even experienced public speakers admit that they are a bit nervous before speaking in front of an audience. In reality, a experiencing a little nervous feeling can actually provide the extra lift that will make your presentation shine.

- Before you start your speech, you will have some time to prepare your material. Use this time to tell yourself that you are really prepared and nothing is going to disrupt you.

- Before you begin speaking, take a few deep breaths to calm your nerves.

- Memorize your first few sentences so that you can express them clearly.

- It is going to be difficult to keep your audience listening. When this happens, do not panic. Involve them in the action and keep your presentation interesting. This are all techniques to avoid them falling asleep.

- Preserve or renew the interest of your audience with visual aids.

- Never quit! Always keep going on. Your speech will get better along the way and do not underrate your audience because they silently want you to succeed.

Holding the audience's attention

If you want your audience to absorb your points effectively, you have to maintain their attention.

The following helpful tips will help you craft memorable speeches:

- *Connect your topic to the audience's needs.* People are not interested in things which are not related to them personally. For this reason it is important that you present every point directly towards the personal needs and values of your audience.

- *Use clear, vivid language.* You must realize that your audience will definitely become bored quickly when they do not understand you. Always try to use familiar words, short sentences, and concrete examples. Your speech will become completely ineffective when you use words or phrases that no one understands. If you have to discuss intangible ideas in your speech, connect the various abstractions with everyday life examples. However, do not make your speech over simplistic. You just need to eliminate difficult words you do not understand yourself.

- *Explain the relationship between your topic and the ideas your audience already knows.* Showing how your topic is related to the ideas the audience already knows which will help the members to categorize and remember your points.

The close of the speech

When you have finished discussing your main points, you may be tempted to finish your speech as soon as possible. Avoid this temptation. The close of your speech is almost as important as the beginning because the attention of your audience will peaks at this point. Plan to allocate around 10 percent of the total time devoted to your speech toward the ending.

An effective technique is to make your audience make a final effort to listen is to tell them that you are about to finish. You do not have to say it with complicated words. Just say "in conclusion" or "to sum it all up." You simply want your audience to know that this is the home stretch.

Restating the main points

Once you have captured the attention of your audience, repeat your main idea. Be sure to emphasize the main points of interest again. Your summary here will reassure your audience that they understand what you want them to do or think. In Addition, you state a key motivating factor relevant to your audience. Reinforce your theme by repeating your main supporting points. A few sentences are generally enough to refresh people's memories.

Outlining the next steps

If you are presenting doing a speech which will require your audience to reach a decision or agree to take specific action, you need to implement a clear wrap-up. In case your audience has agreed on an issue covered in your speech, review the consensus in a sentence or two. If not, take out possible hostile reactions by saying something like "We seem to have some fundamental disagreement on this question." Then go on to suggest a method of resolving the differences.

Ending on a positive note

Ending your speech enthusiastically and memorably is always advisable. Even if you had to present a downbeat speech, try to close on a positive note. Your listeners will always appreciate it when you stress the benefits of action or express confidence in their ability to accomplish the work ahead. Alternatively, you can also end with a question or a statement that will leave your audience thinking.

Remember that your final words will have a big impact on the impression you want to make with your speech. You want to leave your audience with a satisfied feeling: a feeling of completeness. Always avoid introducing new ideas or altering the mood of your audience in the close. Although you want to close on a positive note, try to do it in a natural way and avoid a staged finale.

The question-and-answer Period

Along with the introduction, body, and close, include in your speech time for a question and answer session. Otherwise, writing a report would be much more efficient and effective. A main advantage of delivering a speech is the opportunity to interact with your audience. Do not waste this chief advantage. As a general rule, you may answer questions during your speech if you are addressing a small group, but ask a large audience to safe their questions until you are finished with your speech.

Strangely enough, many excellent speakers do well delivering a speech, but then they falter during the question-and-answer period. The key technique to handle this segment properly is preparation! A lot of speakers simply forget to spend time before delivering a speech to think about the questions that might arise including abrasive or difficult questions. For this reason it is important to prepare yourself with the answers for these questions and more. In fact, some experts recommend that you hold back some dramatic statistics as ammunition for the question-and-answer portion of your speech. However, also realize that circumstances may require you to change the answers you prepared.

Try to give everyone a chance to participate and ask members of your audience sitting in different parts of the room. Do not allow one or two people to monopolize the question and answer period. If the same person continues to demand your attention, address the situation by saying "Sorry, other people might have questions; I'll get back to you if time permits."

Try to maintain control of the situation when an audience member tries to turn a question into an opportunity to mount their own soapboxes. There are three methods to deal with this situation: (1) You might admit that you and the questioner have a difference of opinion and offer to get back to the questioner after you have done more research. Then ask someone else to pose a question; (2) You can offer a brief answer in order to avoid lengthy additional questions; (3) Finally, you might thank the person for the question and then remind the questioner that you were not looking to indulge in put-downs: this may backfire and make your audience sympathize with the questioner.

Avoid going into an argument at all cost! Arguments will definitely cause you to overreact because you feel that your ideas, logic, or facts are being challenged. Stay calm and defuse hostility by applying the following technique: paraphrase the question and ask the questioner to confirm that you have understood it correctly. In case of long complicated questions, break it into parts which you can answer satisfactorily. Always give honest, accurate and factual responses before moving on to the next question. Avoid body language (posture or gestures) that might be perceived as aggression or inapproachability. Keep your tone of voice pleasant and businesslike pleasant (see public speaking checklist below).

The visual aids

If you give a speech without making it visual, your audience will only remember around 10 percent of your message. Your audience will definitely remember more information when your speech is supported with supportive visual aids like slides or overhead transparencies.

Designing and presenting visual aids

Two types of visual aids are used to supplement speeches: text visuals and graphic visuals. The advantage of text visuals which consist of words is that your audience will be able to follow the flow of your ideas because text visuals are simplified outlines of your speech. You can use them to summarize and preview the message and signal major shifts in thought. Graphic visual aids, in turn, help illustrate your main points. They help your audience understand numerical data and other information that would be hard to follow if only presented orally. Think about the visual aids that you will need while preparing the speech or presentation. Select the visual aid which would most benefit your concept.

Simplicity is the key criterion to effectiveness when designing both types of visual aids. Realize that your audience will not be able read and listen at the same time. For this reason, the visual aids have to be simple enough so that the audience can understand them within a moment or two. At the same time, visual aids should be just that, aids that enhance your speech by explaining and emphasizing key points. Too many or too hastily visuals can detract your message.

Most speakers start their speech with several text visuals: the first visual is usually the title page. The title page identifies the topic and signals your audience that the presentation is under way. The second typically lists the three or four major points you' will be covering like a 'road map' of what is to come. The other text visuals will function as aids in emphasizing the transitions between the main points. They are similar to the headings in a written report signaling the introduction of a new topic.

When you present visual ideas, make sure that your audience has the chance to read what is there. Moreover, you also want them to listen to your explanation:

- Make your visual aids large enough so the audience can see them clearly without strain.

- Give your audience time to read a visual aid before you begin your explanation.

- Each visual aid contains only one idea.

- Use visual aids to just illustrate the main points.

- Make sure that your visual aid does not conflict with your verbal message.

- Summarize instead of reading the text of your visual aid word for word.

- After finishing discussing the point illustrated by the visual aid, move on to the next point.

Remember that you want the audience to listen to you, not to study the visual aids. The visual aids are there to increase understanding, do not let them distract your audience.

Selecting the right medium

When you prepare your speech, select one or two of the following visual aids. You have to determine which ones are the best. It depends on the topic of your speech. Simple and straightforward topics only need one visual aid whereas complicated topics might need two aids like slides and handouts.

- *Handouts.*

- *Chalkboards and whiteboards.*

- *Flip chart.*

- *Overheads.*
- *Slides.*
- *Computers.*
- *Other visual aids.*

Public speaking checklist

A. Development of the Speech or Presentation

1. Think about your audience. Who are they?
2. Start a sentence which will attract the attention.
3. Preview the main points.
4. Keep the discussion to a minimal three of four points.
5. Explain the 5W1H (who, what, when, where, why, and how).
6. In case of a longer speech include previews and summaries of major points.
7. Close by repeating your main points and stating something memorable.

B. Visual

1. Use visual aids to make you speech interesting.
2. Use visual aids to highlight important information.
3. Select appropriate visual aids.
   a. For small groups, use flip charts, boards, or transparencies
   b. For large groups, use slides or film.
4. Limit slide or transparency to five or six points.
5. Use short sentences.
6. Use large and readable letters.
7. Check the equipment before to make sure it works.

C. Delivery

1. Keep eye contact.
2. Speak clearly.
3. Do not go too fast or too slow.
4. Be sure everyone can hear you (check sound system)
5. Speak naturally and use your normal tone of voice.
6. Do not slough.
7. Demonstrate natural gestures.
8. Invite questions.
   a. If the group is small, it is ok to answer questions during your speech.
   b. If the group is large, ask your audience to hold their questions until the end.

9. Focus on answering one question at a time.

10. When facing criticism, stay calm and control your feelings.

BIBLIOGAPHY

Blair, Kendall, *The Most Important Questions to Ask on Your Next Job Interview, Insider Secrets You Need to Know,* 2007, Florida, USA.

Bovée, C. L., Thill, J. V., *Business Communication Today,* 1995, 4th, McGraw-Hill, New York.

Burns, R., *Doing Business in Asia, A Cultural Perspective,* 1998, Longman, Melbourne

Cole, K., Crystal *Clear Communication, Skills for Understanding and Being Understood,* 1993, 2nd, Synergy Books, Kuala Lumpur.

Dudley, G. A.,*Your Personality and How to Use It Effectively,* 1996, S.S. Mubaruk & Brothers, Singapore.

Dwyer, J., *The Business Communication Handbook,* 1997, 4th, Prentice Hall, Sydney.

Elias Norbert, *The Civilizing Process,* 2000, 2nd, Wiley-Blackwell, Oxford.

Goldberg, M., Insider's *Guide to the 9 Personality Types, The Enneagram for Success at Work,* 1997, Thorsons, London.

Gordon, J. R., *Organizational behavior, A Diagnostic Approach,* 1998, 6th, Prentice Hall, New Jersey.

Habermas, J., *The Theory of Communicative Action, Volume One, Reason and the Rationalization of Society,* 1984, Heinemann, London.

Habermas, J., *The Theory of Communicative Action, Volume Two, Lifeworld and System: A Critique of Functionalist Reason,* 1987, Beacon Press, Boston.

Hostede, G., *Cultures and Organizations, Software of the Mind,* 1991, McGraw-Hill, London.

Liaw, P, *Understanding Your Communication Styles,* 2005, Elex Media Komputindo, Jakarta.

Rokeach, F. M., The Nature and Meaning of Dogmatism, in *Psychological Review,* 61, 1960, p.19-204.

Hamlin, S., *How to Talk so People Listen,* 2006, Harper Collins, New York.

Tubbs, S. L., Moss, S., *Human Communication: An Interpersonal Perspective*, 1974, Random House, New York.